Al Allen gives us an insightful narrative of profound life experiences that have transformed his spiritual perspective and clarified his purpose in life. Most importantly, this engaging and well-written book can help readers along their own personal path of revelation.

— John Z. Amoroso, Ph.D., Clinical Psychologist, author of *Awakening Past Lives*

The author takes the reader on an emotional roller coaster as he relates his multiple life-threatening and life-enhancing experiences. Such events, often unexplainable, defy his science background but ultimately lead to the discovery of his life's purpose. We are reminded that profound answers are often revealed as clues within our own experiences and relationships.

— Dale Megill, author of *A Footbridge to the Light*

CLUES CAN LIGHT THE WAY

A DISCOVERY OF CLUES FOR THE GREATEST PUZZLE OF ALL: THE PURPOSE OF LIFE AND BEYOND

Alan A. Allen

Archway Publishing books may be ordered through booksellers or by contacting:

Archway Publishing
1663 Liberty Drive
Bloomington, IN 47403
www.archwaypublishing.com
844-669-3957

Because of the dynamic nature of the Internet, any web addresses or
links contained in this book may have changed since publication and
may no longer be valid. The views expressed in this work are solely those
of the author and do not necessarily reflect the views of the publisher,
and the publisher hereby disclaims any responsibility for them.

Interior Image Credit: Robert C. Ellis

ISBN: 978-1-4808-9515-7 (sc)
ISBN: 978-1-4808-9514-0 (hc)
ISBN: 978-1-4808-9516-4 (e)

Library of Congress Control Number: 2020916360

Print information available on the last page.

Archway Publishing rev. date: 11/05/2020

This book is dedicated to my parents, Edith Marie and Charles Peter Allen. They gave to me the unconditional love and freedom to live life fully, make mistakes, discover my potential, and explore the purpose of my life.

Acknowledgements

This book would not have been possible without the support and encouragement of my family and so many good friends. They frequently suggested that I document the many stories I shared with them of childhood events, travels abroad, and experiences with totally unexplainable outcomes. My daughter Lauren, my sons Matthew and Andrew, and their spouses have also provided valuable input as reviewers and advisors for the book's content and illustrations.

I would also like to acknowledge the valuable support of my son Chris, who provided encouragement for the writing of this book right up until his passing at the age of forty-five from cancer.

My wife Anda is that very special person who needs to be given credit for not only supporting the writing and review of this book, but for the decades of witnessing many of the events and impacts of the incidents described in it. With a master's degree in library science and a keen eye for correct grammar, she insisted on accuracy in both my recall of an event and its description.

It is with great pleasure that I acknowledge the help of a very good friend and business associate that I have worked with for several decades. Mr. James Lukin is a highly experienced writer and editor, having worked extensively for industry, government, and academic institutions for over forty-five years. Mr. Lukin contributed invaluable time and energy in helping to organize and edit this book. Because of his familiarity with the life and travels of the author, his input provided unique personal guidance for the content and reader-friendly nature of the book.

Mr. Robert Ellis, also a close friend, is a recognized artist and professional illustrator, having worked for many businesses, academic organizations, magazines, and other publishing groups. He has worked with the author of this book on numerous technical manuals, training materials, and project reports, using his skills to produce a variety of hand-drawn sketches, portraits, and images. Mr. Ellis was instrumental in creating the cover for this book and the images at the start of each chapter.

Besides family and friends acknowledged above, the Institute of Noetic Sciences (IONS) has played a significant role in helping me recognize the importance of writing this book. Created in 1973 by Apollo 14 astronaut Dr. Edgar Mitchell, IONS provides reliable, carefully researched information on the connection between science and mind. My recognition of the importance of things considered provable, along with those that might be a bit "spooky," was helped along by the insight of Dr. Mitchell and the commitment of IONS scientists to explore consciousness and a myriad of unexplainable phenomena. The research and findings of IONS over nearly five decades have given me the courage to explore and document the mysterious events of my own life and to explore its purpose.

Contents

Introduction

It is exciting to be eighty-two years old in the year 2020, a year that might suggest a clarity or sharpness of vision. And I now believe I have reached a clear vision of my life's purpose and want to share my journey to that clarity.

For the first forty years of my life, I thought I could see and appreciate my life as a journey with incredibly exciting events. Some of those experiences were youthful, fun-filled adventures when life was simple and risk was rarely an issue. Others involved situations where the risks of serious injury or death were there, sometimes realized, rarely taken seriously, and often forgotten.

During that phase of my life, there were also times when mysterious, unexplainable events occurred and captured my attention. Those events were unforgettable and have profoundly influenced me. Some involved circumstances and outcomes so unexplainable that I could only interpret their significance as guidance from an *all-knowing source beyond this world*. My closest, most religious friends said that it was God or guardian angels that had spared my life, while others, especially my atheist friends, said I was just lucky. But these accidents and other close encounters with death felt like clues to the path I should follow in my life and what my life purpose could be.

My confusion over the cause and effects of those incidents and any possible divine intervention is not surprising. My father was a non-practicing Protestant; my mother was Catholic, removed from the church when she married my dad; and they sent me as a child to the nearest place of worship, a Baptist church. This upbringing and continued brief encounters with religion often felt comforting, but not convincing. There were signs along the way that gave me hope about a path I had yet to discover, but I could not see the way. In my early years I found the greatest satisfaction and confidence with the precision of mathematics and science.

The delayed recognition and acceptance of potentially life-changing events were undoubtedly tied to my sixty-year career as a scientist involved with nuclear physics, petroleum engineering, oceanography, and marine biology. My degree in physics and several years of advanced graduate study provided opportunities to teach, manage organizations, develop patents, publish research papers, and conduct field investigations in dozens of countries.

I was comfortable and confident with the scientific process of experimentation, quantitative assessment and analysis, and proof of data or theories through controlled, repeatable tests. Events that could not be explained—that could not be measured and plugged into an equation—were fascinating and exciting, but they could not provide the evidence I needed to cross that frightening, rapid river of doubt and confusion. I wanted a strong, undeniable experience that would provide the clarity of vision and understanding to help light my path of self-discovery and purpose. That experience happened as I approached the mid-life stage (so far) of my time on earth.

The most uplifting, life-changing encounter with the unexplainable involved my father's transition from life to death and back. His heart stopped at age sixty-five while he and my mother were living in Leonardo, New Jersey, where I grew up. At the local hospital, my father was pronounced clinically dead for about eight minutes. Chapter 10, "Love and Learn," describes his passage out of his body, through a tunnel, and into the most beautiful place he said he had ever been. I describe how a *knowing*—a strong emotional directive—led me to go home to New Jersey from Alaska. After considerable disbelief and attempts to ignore the directive, I went anyway and then learned that my father had died earlier but had come back.

To my amazement, he was not surprised by my arrival, seemingly aware of a request for me to do so. Describing his experience, he told me of a reunion with his brother who had died earlier that year. He spoke of how a brilliant light behind his brother communicated telepathically with clear messages of love and understanding. What he learned changed his outlook on life and why we come to earth. I could see that my father was no longer the grumpy, lonely, and depressed man I had known most of my life; and he spoke with love and appreciation of me. We discussed our many misunderstandings and hard feelings, and it was wonderful to reach a happy closure on those issues. About a month after I returned to Alaska, my father died, and I was so glad for the time we shared during that last visit.

My father gave me a new perspective on the close calls I had experienced to that point in my life. Each event—the frightening ones and the enlightening ones—became an example for how I could better appreciate the path I was on. I began to see the lessons from each experience as clues about the value of every person. The connections with people and the help we can provide for each other became paramount. It became increasingly clear that my ability to grow spiritually did not depend on proof of concept and validation with mathematics and science.

I grew to appreciate more than ever that I am not just my physical body and that the survival of consciousness after death need not be proven. The personal stories I have selected from my own life journey and provided in this book leave me satisfied with simply the *likelihood* that each of us is part of something so very much greater than ourselves—a perfect expression of love.

Nothing we ever think, say, or do can change what lies beyond this world. In a very real sense, it is comforting beyond measure to know that:

Whatever is, just simply Is…

1

Earliest Close Calls

This two-part chapter deals with the very first bad decisions I can remember that resulted in injury and apparently no lessons learned. Since these events happened at the ages of two and five, it is not surprising that I cannot remember the details. However, they help set the stage for an appreciation of how I managed to get into trouble so many ways the rest of my life and to be here today to write about them.

My reason for sharing these experiences is *not* to suggest that any one of us is more worthy of life than another or that there is a divine plan from which we cannot stray. I believe that all individuals have the capacity to make their own decisions, to live and learn from them, and to decide for themselves if there is purpose and maybe even guidance through it all. In my case, the lessons learned and any purpose for them were slow in coming, as was my eventual awakening to the possibility of guidance from beyond this world.

As with the two vaguely remembered events described here, it seems that my path in life was almost intended to involve risks, miraculous survivals, and fortunately, many wonderful low-risk encounters. It would be decades before I began to recognize these events as *clues* from which I could discover a path filled with opportunities to learn.

Cookies and Coffee

When I was a toddler approaching two years of age, it was already clear to my parents that I had to be watched closely. If the lid of a trunk could be opened, I'd climb in; if stairs or a ladder could be found, I'd soon be at the top with no fear or experience in getting down; and if a door was cracked open, I'd have to know what was behind it. I am told that when I first started to reach for doorknobs, all exits and forbidden rooms had to have toddler-proof means of opening them.

One morning my sweet mama left me alone for a few minutes to finish my breakfast. It was just enough time for me to explore a small pantry door that had been left ajar. I have absolutely no memory of this exciting excursion.

Grownups later surmised that I must have pushed on the inward swinging door, entered, and somehow pushed the door back to its fully closed and latched position.

I am told that I must have sat on the floor for hours, quietly devouring the contents of a box of chocolate chip cookies. With only a narrow band of light from beneath the door, and a full tummy, I was apparently ready for a nap upon a comfy sack of flour nearby. The panicky search by my mom throughout the house and the frantic hunt by neighbors simply went unheard by this dozing desperado. When they finally checked that tiny pantry closet and found me fast asleep in a pile of cookie crumbs, I suspect there was the usual mixed emotions of *RAGE* (*relief, anger, gladness, and elation*) when a missing child is found!

Now for the catastrophe with coffee, which fortunately at two years of age, I do not remember either! I am told that while gathering for breakfast with family one morning, I had been crawling around beneath the kitchen table. As everyone took their seats, I was told to come out and take my seat as well. All the food had been prepared, and fresh coffee had just been brewed in a percolator. The details of this story have likely become somewhat muddled through the years. However, I am told that someone moved the coffee pot from the stove and placed it on an insulating pad to protect the table and its tablecloth. The tablecloth added a nice touch for the breakfast, but it also hung several inches over the sides of the table.

The outcome is painfully easy to imagine. Yes, as I crawled out from beneath the table, the tablecloth was just too close and convenient. Pulling on it to help get on my feet, I managed to pull the cloth and the coffee pot over the edge of the table spilling most of its contents over me. I suffered significant burns over my head, back, and legs. The damage was worsened by the immediate saturation of my clothing and perhaps only a marginal awareness of appropriate first aid.

After I spent several days at a local hospital, the doctors and nurses were pleased with the healing taking place; and I went home. I have only faint, fragmented memories from the time I spent in the hospital. They are brief, dream-like wisps of recall involving hazy images and feelings of discomfort and fear, rather than scenes, people, or discussions.

No lessons learned from the cookie and coffee events! I do remember, however, that I never stopped loving cookies, while finding the smell of coffee disgusting! Later, in chapter 4, "Thin Ice," I reveal a brush with death that resulted in my discovery and lasting love of a good hot cup of coffee.

High on Candy, Short on Patience

When I was five years old living with my parents in Kearny, New Jersey, life seemed simple and secure. Being a kid during the early 1940s had its perks. My parents seemed to have sufficient confidence that I could safely play unsupervised for short periods in front of our apartment building with other kids on my block. My memory of the rules for such freedom are vague; however, I apparently stayed away from the street and was always within view of our apartment windows a few floors up.

A few times a week my mother would walk with me to a nearby intersection with traffic lights. When the light turned green, she would take my hand and hurry to the opposite corner where a small store had the most unbelievable display of candies any five-year-old would die for. Yup, as you can imagine, I almost did! Heck, in those days you could get a handful of goodies for just a penny. Who would not take a little risk for such a treasure?!

One day, sitting alone on the steps to our apartment building, I spied a penny lying unclaimed on the sidewalk. What a find! I would like to believe that I paused as I picked it up and thought about that penny's original sad owner, or how happy my mother would be if I brought it to her. No! I suspect that I hid it quickly in my pocket, dreamed of the sweet treasures it could buy, and checked the apartment window to see if my mom was watching. After all, I had lots of experience with the intersection and its lights just a block from home.

The memories of my first serious temptation with money are of course hazy. However, I do remember running to the intersection, dashing across the street with a group of people as the light turned green, and racing into that glorious candy store. The owner, I suspect, must have thought that my mother was briefly out of sight as he exchanged that penny for a handful of my favorite sugar-rich gems. I quickly left the store, ran to the crosswalk, checked the traffic lights, and looked around for a friendly escort.

The excitement of financing my own first purchase of candy must have been overwhelming! I suspect that I was still looking for an escort when the light turned green. By the time I turned and saw the green light, I must have thought I could make it across the intersection. Lacking the wisdom and patience to wait, I started at top speed into the intersection. The world, as I knew it, went blank. Feeling no pain, no fear, no anything, I remember opening my eyes briefly, lying on the back seat of a vehicle next to a bag of groceries that had tipped over spilling its contents. A few bananas lay within inches of my face. Funny how the memory of those bananas sticks in my brain after all these years, and how I wanted to reach for them and take a bite. I could not move, and I suspect that I passed out again, coming to in the hospital.

The events of my brief stay at the hospital are vague. All I know is that my parents had called the police when I was discovered missing and that they were able to locate me and bring me home. I suffered only bruises and a few minor scratches. The healing of my body went quickly, but the recovery from that scare (maybe *RAGE*) left my parents struggling with their decision to live in the city.

Within that year, we moved to the small town of Leonardo, New Jersey, with a small railroad station, post office, grocery store, church, and a bar. It was a perfect place to grow up because it was located near a grade school and high school, had lots of woods to play in, and was a short walk to the ocean. I stayed there with my folks, my older brother, and a sister who arrived when I was fifteen. I laugh now at the embarrassment I felt when friends found out that my mom was pregnant. Back then, it was unbelievable, even disgusting, to think that older people in their forties still "Do it!" Yuk! Well, the years flew by; and I graduated from Middletown Township High School in 1956 and Washington & Jefferson College, Washington, Pennsylvania, in 1960.

Little did I know that by the time I was twenty-one years old, I would have already experienced several close encounters with death and unexplainable survival from each event. Those close calls never seemed to be that big a deal. I was too busy with school and trying to put my education to use. My enjoyment of mathematics and science completely filled my world of learning and left little room for thoughts of any purpose for my life.

It took another twenty years of challenges, failures, successes, and paradoxical events for me to appreciate that some of life's most important lessons need not be proven with science, or even fully understood. Those events and lessons became the *clues* that gradually revealed a path of discovery and a purpose for my life. This book is not only a summary of events along that path; it is the fulfillment of a personal goal to share the results of that journey.

2

A Day at The Beach

The move from Newark to Leonardo, New Jersey, was a wonderful relocation for the Allen family. We were now enjoying the peace and comfort of a small town near the ocean. So comfortable were my folks that they rarely ever locked the door to our home; and by the time I was eight years old, they had even let me head for the beach on my own. As I remember, the only instruction I received was "be good, and be home by five for supper." This confidence in me was appreciated, but it nearly did me in!

I had mastered the art of floating on water while kicking and thrashing my arms sufficiently to move forward. Most of this skill came about as my buddies and I played water-tag in the nearshore shallow waters. With time, we got brave enough to jump off an old wooden jetty that reached out from the beach to a water depth of about six feet at high tide. We usually had enough sense to stay close to the jetty as the tide came in.

As with most kids at that age, my confidence grew faster than my sense of good judgment. Toward the end of the summer, I could dive into water over my head, wiggle, thrash around underwater, and come up a good fifteen to twenty feet away. Gasping, but with enough dignity to act in control, I would manage to turn around and thrash my way back to the jetty. I was thoroughly enjoying another phase of my life that seemed safe and yet fast, fun, and fearless.

It wasn't long before I expanded my beach activities to include fishing from a pier nearby and testing my skills with a wooden slingshot I had made. It felt good, having made my own bamboo fishing pole and a slingshot I could use to scare seagulls off the pier! I was developing a good eye and a masterful sling until the day I succeeded in hitting a small sandpiper. That little bird was happily darting back and forth between waves, looking for food in the wet sand. Amazed that I could actually hit such a small, fast-moving target, I rushed to inspect the results of my first hunt.

That sorrowful little bird twisted and quivered without a sound in the palm of my hand. I just could not handle its final glance toward me as it died. It was a heart-breaking emotional experience for me to witness a life cut short because of a thoughtless, stupid decision on my part. I hoped that my buddies would not see me crying as I buried that lifeless little bird in the sand.

Only eight years old, but the lessons kept on coming. It was only a few days later when I decided to grab my fishing pole and head for the beach. The day started, I am certain, without a care in the world, and with the usual peanut-butter sandwich and carrot sticks Mom always packed for me. Little did I know that I was about to learn, once again, how poor decisions can lead to serious life-threatening results—even my own life!

After a great swim with my friends at the jetty, we would scarf down our snacks and race to the only public drinking-water fountain near the beach. It didn't matter at all that the water was warm and tasted a bit rusty. Then there was that long, mile walk from our usual swim site all the way around the marina to one of our favorite fishing spots at the entrance to the harbor. It seemed especially long as we ran barefoot, yelping and laughing with pain, over endless stretches of hot pavement and sharp gravel.

Once we got to the other side of the harbor's entrance, we would dig up some worms, stick one on a hook, and lower that poor little critter into the water. It didn't really matter if the snappers were biting that day or not! Half of the fun was watching the boats come and go at the entrance to the marina, picking the one we'd someday own, or stopping now and then to see who could find the best cloud-figure drifting overhead. Mixed in were deep philosophical debates about the pain that worms must feel, whether it was better to drown or be eaten alive, and if God might punish us for killing worms.

My sweet mom, then in her mid-thirties, also loved the beach. This particular day she had come down for a swim and some sun while we were fishing on the other side of the harbor's entrance. With only a fifty- to sixty-foot-wide channel separating us, I could see my mother relaxing on the beach. And, as the dinner-hour approached, I remember her picking up her blanket and towel, and moving toward my location. My buddies had already pulled in their empty hooks and were starting back around the harbor as I tried to capture just a few more minutes and perhaps the only fish of the day.

As Mom approached the edge of the channel, I could see a bunch of teenagers diving in from the other side and playing in the channel between us. The noise level was pretty high as they screamed and cannonballed each other between the passing of boats.

As I twirled the string around my bamboo fishing pole and secured the hook at one end, I couldn't help thinking about how close the other channel wall seemed. The upper edge of the wall was about ten feet above the water at mid-tide, and it had a single ladder built into it. I could hardly stand the temptation to jump in and swim to the other side. How neat it would be, I thought, to spare my feet the uncomfortable long walk back around the harbor and to show my mom just how good a swimmer I had become. The distance to the other side did not worry me. There were no incoming or outgoing boats in view, and I was sure I could swim the fifty to sixty feet, pushing my pole ahead of me.

The excitement of the challenge, unimpeded by the weight of wisdom, seemed a reasonable risk. I knew there was a tidal current through that channel at times, but I also saw others swimming near the wall on the other side. If they could do it, so could I!

Signaling to my mother to wait there, I quickly threw my pole into the water and dove in after it. I am sure I was careful not to look back at her as I prepared to dive. Given the chance, she surely would have disapproved of my plan. Too late! The dive was perfect, and I am sure I must have felt a sense of pride as I entered the water.

After surfacing, I began swimming toward the other side, pushing my pole ahead of me. Within seconds I could tell that I was drifting seaward out of the harbor entrance at a fairly good rate. The tide was going out, and so was I! Feeling a bit anxious about the situation, I soon abandoned my fishing pole and started swimming harder. I also changed my direction and started swimming with a greater angle upstream.

I must have swum like crazy for what seemed an eternity. With near-panic strokes, I finally reached an area fairly close to where the big kids had been playing. I was breathing hard and starting to take in small gulps of water, when I realized I just could not swim the last ten feet or so to the jetty wall. I hated to give in and call for help, but I knew I no longer had a choice.

Thrashing and kicking to stay afloat, I suddenly bumped into one of the older boys who had been playing near the jetty. It was all I could do to squeak out a pretty feeble "help" while throwing an arm over his shoulder to keep from slipping below the surface. Unfortunately, the guy must have thought I was just another kid from his group. He reached back and gave me a good push underwater. The water was dark and cold as I slipped down deeper in the channel. Slivers of light reaching down from the surface gave me the direction for another attempt to resurface and find air.

My last memory involves a brief vision of the sky, an attempt to breathe, and the sound of kids laughing and screaming nearby. This fraction of relief, however, was abruptly ended as I felt a hand push me underwater again. With so little air remaining in my lungs, the possible intake of water, and no energy left, I could have easily passed out and slipped down well below the surface. The noise and excitement of kids splashing and dunking each other should have been interrupted, I would think, by the screams of a panicked mother. To this day, however, I still do not know what went on while I was drowning or shortly thereafter.

It was as if an interval of time had been stolen—as if waking from a nightmare, I was suddenly walking slowly and calmly with my mom along the roadside leading back to our home. It was as if nothing had ever happened. Neither my mother nor I spoke of the drowning or of being saved.

As best I can remember, I had no physical or emotional discomfort as we walked quietly together. There was no discussion of my attempt to swim the channel, no scolding for my failure to anticipate the strong current, and no discomfort or soreness in my throat or lungs. There was no discussion of heroic moves to lift me out of the channel or of anyone clearing water from my lungs. In fact, it must have been a day or two later when the memory of drowning flooded back into my consciousness.

When I brought up the subject with my mother, she simply looked at me for a few seconds and turned away. I thought she was mad at me for doing something so stupid. It must have been weeks before I brought it up again, and when I did, she appeared very uneasy and said something about not understanding what had happened. Once, she admitted having seen me struggle in the water, but that is the last thing she could remember.

Every once in a while, I would think about that day at the beach. I could recall everything clearly until I was going down below the surface that second time. It was as if the missing critical interval of time had been erased.

A few years later, I wrote a school paper about the near drowning and the gap in time. My friends and teacher thought I had made up the story.

My mom had little patience with things she could not understand. For both my mother and me, there was a totally unexplainable period of time during which we could not account for the words or actions of us or anyone else that may have witnessed my brush with death. My mother politely insisted that we never talk about it again. The event remained a mystery, never again spoken of with her, and shared only with close friends and relatives.

3

A Push in the Dark

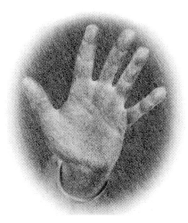

This is a short story about a short guy on a short walk just a short distance from his home. I was only ten years old, but quite comfortable walking the three blocks to my good friend's home day or night. That friend, Bob Megill, would become a truly best friend; and we would share the title of best man at each other's wedding. Bob was that special person every kid should have to share the ups and downs of youth. We were always there for each other when the road got bumpy or when it could have taken us in a bad direction.

One night, the road got especially bumpy as I headed over to Bob's home after dinner. It was already dark, so I was careful to walk in the gravel and dirt shoulders of that narrow, paved road. Homes along the way were set back about twenty to thirty feet from the road, with crab grass, weeds, and sometimes a dirt path or steppingstones from the gravel shoulder to the house. Scraggly old bushes and trees were common along the edge of the road, objects behind which my mind could envision all kinds of creatures ready to attack.

The path to Bob's house during the day was a friendly route with typical family activities going on and plenty to keep one's mind filled with happy thoughts of a new bike, baseball games, or a design for the next tree fort. What a great time to be a kid in the 1940s—not a single thought about drugs, computer games, or even television.

Nighttime was another story! I was afraid of the dark till I was about twelve—well, maybe a little longer. But since my mom and dad didn't seem concerned about my walking to Bob's home after dark, what could there be to worry about?! Hmm, there were probably just as many drunks, kidnappers, and weirdos back then as there are today—they just didn't get much publicity, so it seemed a lot safer to be out alone.

As I walked toward Bob's home that night, it never entered my mind that a danger greater than any monster behind the bushes could be an approaching sleepy or drunken driver. I should have been more mindful that night of such a possibility. With only a block or two to go,

I remember hearing the engine of a car approaching from behind. It was quite a way back and gave me no cause for concern. As the car got closer, I was somewhat thankful for its headlights because I could see, for a minute, the trees, bushes, and objects ahead. I was, no doubt, carefully checking the shadows (and anything in them) as the vehicle approached.

The car seemed to be traveling normally, and there was no reason to look back over my shoulder. The car's engine noise, lights, and route on the road gave no reason for concern until the last few seconds before it reached me. I suddenly sensed an unusual intensity of the car's lights directly on my back. Also, my own shadow was not moving to the side as it should; and in an instant, there was the sound of tires spraying dirt and gravel right behind me. Jerking my head quickly to look behind me, I had not even completed my turn, when out of nowhere, something pushed hard and firmly on my shoulder. I was knocked, head over heels, sideways off the shoulder of the road, rolling to a stop in someone's front yard. I jumped up in time to catch a glimpse of the car's taillights as it swerved wildly back onto the narrow, paved road and sped away.

Confused and shaken, I remember thinking something like: "Holy shit! What just happened?!" I knew I had not been hit by the car. It felt like someone's hand had pushed me off the shoulder of the road a fraction of a second before the car screeched through the spot where I had been standing. I simply brushed myself off and walked on toward Bob's home. Later that night I told him that the strangest thing happened to me on the way over to his place. We probably pondered about it for a few minutes, laughed, and thought "Wow, that's weird," and then went back to just being ten.

I will end this story with a profound statement made by another ten-year-old boy, my youngest son, about the dark. We were sharing feelings one night about people that are afraid of the dark. At one point I asked him if he was afraid of the dark. He quickly replied: "No, I'm not afraid of the dark. I'm afraid of what's in the dark!"

Over the next few years, I seemed to follow a fairly uneventful path with no serious injuries or close calls with the gloomy grim reaper. There were times when I did push the envelope—setting a field on fire (and almost a row of homes and myself) while playing with matches; escaping from the car of a would-be abductor while hitchhiking; and falling about thirty feet from a tree fort to the ground, lying there alone and unconscious until waking, barely able to breath or move for quite a while. These events, like the mystical push in the dark, are clearly memorable; but none was sufficient at that time to inspire such questions as: Why was I spared? Is there a purpose for which I am still alive?

4

Thin Ice

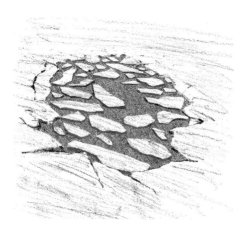

On two occasions as a teenager, I failed to avoid thin ice. You'd think a sixteen-year-old would remember what happened at fifteen! These frightening brushes with death took place while ice skating, one in the middle of the day on a lake, the other at night on a river. The locations and conditions were different, but the results were the same, and both times fate failed to take me down. To this day I wonder if it was adrenaline, luck, or maybe something more that stepped in and saved my frigid butt!

A Day on Lake Ice

As curious, fun-seeking kids, my friends and I often spent the cold winter weekends searching for frozen ponds or streams where we could race each other on skates, see who could jump the farthest, or play hockey. We would spend an entire day clearing leaves, sticks, and junk from a frozen pond, and then have the greatest fun with a broken tree limb for a hockey stick and a stone for a puck. Those were the days when kids seemed to have more time to be creative and spend lots of time outdoors. Television was not available to many; and drugs, alcohol, and portable phones had no place in our lives. It was great being a kid! However, this did not mean that we were free from danger, careless behavior, and plain ole stupid decisions.

One of my most stupid ideas came about after finding a lake in the woods where we had never skated. It was bigger than any we had ever seen in the area, and the ice was smooth with few leaves and sticks to get in our way. A small farmhouse and a barn existed at one end of the lake, while large evergreen trees surrounded the rest of this beautiful frozen playground.

We quickly rounded up suitable hockey "sticks," flat-rock pucks, and some small logs to serve as goals. After a couple of hours of the usual bumps, bruises, and brutal accusations of foul play, it was time for a break. The best break might include a tree stump for a seat, clean snow for dry mouths, and a crumpled sandwich or candy bar stashed away by a thoughtful mom.

As energy returned to the gang of rock-flicking future hockey stars, discussions soon turned to some favorite contests involving races and long jumps. For the jumps we would set two logs parallel to each other, with each of us skating at top speed in an effort to clear them both. The space between the logs would be increased until each competitor had been eliminated after three failed attempts. Needless to say, injuries and/or lack of courage to try again usually eliminated players quite fast!

As logs were being rounded up, I told the group I would join in but that I just wanted to explore the other end of the lake first. Before anyone could complain or offer to join me, I was off and cruising at a rather good pace. I was curious to see what the ice was like at the far end of the lake. Besides, it should only take a few minutes to reach the lake's edge about a quarter of a mile away. The issue of ice strength never entered my mind since the ice that day seemed to be in excess of six to eight inches.

Hmm, it turns out I had not yet learned that streams feeding into a body of water may be a bit warmer at the surface near their entrance and that currents and turbulence can slow down ice formation. Even if I had known that, it is likely that I never would have noticed a couple of streams fed by warmer groundwater entering the lake straight ahead. The smooth rhythm of my push and glide strokes, the enjoyment of the sunny day, the crisp clean air, and the pleasant break from my friends would all, within seconds, be shattered by an unexpected sinking sensation.

It is hard to explain the combination and compression of so many feelings into a split second of time. I do remember, however, my skates stopping suddenly as they broke through thin ice and my body falling forward. There was the shock of sinking fast as ice-cold water splashed up into my face and started soaking through my clothing. A latent fear of becoming completely submerged erupted in my brain. Funny how the last thoughts of drowning at the age of eight come roaring out of one's subconscious when aroused by liquid panic. All of this in an instant was worsened by the reality that I was surrounded by ice and was sinking fast with saturated winter gear, hat, gloves, and ice skates weighing me down.

My first reaction, I recall clearly, was to thrust my soggy body upward to keep my head above water and to swim like hell back toward what had been thick ice. Wrong! My soggy winter clothing and thrashing attempts to get back onto solid ice only resulted in continued saturation of inner clothing and rapid loss of energy and body heat. The surge of adrenaline was of little value as I struggled to climb back up onto the thickest ice while moving away from the lake's shoreline.

That's it! The shoreline! I remember pausing for a few seconds and feeling a presence of calm around and within me. I also felt a sensation of clarity that helped me realize that I was less than a hundred feet from the shoreline. I reversed my direction and took on a sloppy, though somewhat effective, doggy paddle toward the lake's edge.

After a few minutes I realized that I would likely see tomorrow. I heard the cheers of encouragement from my skating buddies behind me, wisely still on solid ice away from my swimming hole. There were also a couple of guys sort of running in their skates along the edge of the lake toward my intended exit. Shortly after that, I felt my own skates contact the bottom of the lake. It was great for a few seconds, until I discovered how hard it is to extract one's skates from the soft mud of a lakebed. Frozen, shivering, and exhausted, I paddled with feet off the bottom, as best I could, until I could crawl out of the water and onto shore.

A true friend will give you the shirt off his back. My friends were truer than true as they offered jackets, hats, gloves, and a lot of help walking me back to that barn we had seen earlier. Fortunately, an old man was working in the barn; and he had a beautiful, hot, wood-burning, potbelly stove he was willing to share. Off came every stitch of clothing. On came some dirty old coveralls and a smelly sweatshirt donated by the potbelly-stove owner. Many funny stories from a kind old man, a lot of swimming-with-skates jokes, and lots of hot chocolate were shared that afternoon.

It took hours for my clothes to dry that day, but it has taken decades to fully appreciate how that icy swim was to be one of many lessons learned by this old coot. Some lessons seem to come slowly to kids from Jersey. But I've discovered that if we live long enough, the lessons start to fit like pieces of a puzzle. Just like a store-bought, premium quality, thousand-piece puzzle, each piece of that puzzle is different. The pieces, with a sufficient number positioned properly, begin to reveal what will become a grand and beautiful picture. In my mid-teens I had no idea of what the picture might look like or that there even was a picture. I must admit that the moment of calm and clarity of thought that came over me in that icy water did stick, engraved in my memory. Such moments were just beginning to take shape as clues or as pieces of a puzzle that were important, though I knew not why. They would gnaw upon my curiosity especially when remembering the fear that I felt in that icy lake when I was sure that my number was up. Little did I know that I must have more than one number!

A Night on River Ice

Only a year had gone by since my frigid swim in broken lake ice. The same group (plus or minus a few members) and I were out for a super fun night on river ice. It was mid-winter with well-below-freezing air temperatures and a clear sky with brilliant stars shining down on not-so-brilliant teenagers.

We had always talked about how much fun it would be to skate at night. We also wanted to drive (I now had a driver's license!) a bit farther to a frozen river, the Navesink River in Red Bank, New Jersey. It was a popular area for swimming and water skiing in summer and for ice skating and ice boating in winter. The event that evening was well planned, parental approval was granted (for some of us), and I even had a new pair of ice skates I was dying to try (whoops, bad choice of words).

We found a great place to park near the river with easy access out onto the ice. There were no other skaters in sight, and it was deadly silent (whoops, again). The ice was pretty smooth, my new skates felt great, and everyone was excited to explore that frozen river from bank to bank. Everything seemed to be moving in a positive direction as we soaked up the joy of being young, healthy, happy, and oblivious.

Yes, we were oblivious to how to safely skate on a river that we had never dealt with before. I knew well, from personal experience, how ice thickness can be affected by relatively warm streams and even subtle turbulence at and beneath ice at the edge of a lake. That night, however, I was totally and literally in the dark regarding the effects on the ice of heat exchange from a low bridge and heavy traffic.

I suspect that you can surmise the event and the outcome of what once again humbled this aggressive, limit-testing speed-demon on ice. It had probably been less than an hour of team exploration over at least a mile or two of that river from bank to bank. Many in our group were tiring and slowing down, a wonderful sign that I could prove my endurance and manliness. Heck, even my dad trusted me to take his car to the next town. Well, maybe he didn't know exactly which town!

It felt so good to rev up my pace and head straight upriver toward the town of Red Bank and the bridge we had used earlier to cross the river. I could see that the river became narrower as I approached the bridge and that ice extended well into a marsh at least a quarter of a mile beyond the bridge. There appeared to be lots of good ice to extend my excursion before heading back to my friends.

Well, it was only a couple of minutes before the memory of a once terrible "daymare" on ice suddenly became a genuine nightmare! It was a totally unexpected plunge through weakened ice and a practically instantaneous submergence of skates, body, and head.

After surfacing, I thrashed about with heavy, wet clothing, trying to find thick, stable ice. I tried to yell out while gagging on smelly river water, but the call was weak and pathetic. I remember feeling embarrassed for a few seconds, hoping that my buddies hadn't seen this Olympian master ice-breaker conduct a repeat performance. The embarrassment, however, was quickly replaced with shear panic and the hope that someone, somehow, saw or heard a splash or garbled cry for help. I knew that I could not depend upon the valuable escape tactics I had learned at the lake a year ago. The river water was deep, the shore was too far away, and the pilings of the bridge were wide, tall, and absent of any surfaces I could grab onto.

I struggled for several seemingly endless minutes, trying to break through thin ice back toward the path I had been on when I went in. By the time I finally reached thicker ice, I was so tired, cold, and saturated that I could not pull myself up onto the ice. With nothing to grab onto, I could only get part of my shoulders out of the water before I'd slip back beneath the water surface. It was at about this point when I remembered the sensation of calm and clarity that had come over me during my last frigid dip. I paused and waited for some kind of divine intervention and solution to my dilemma. Nothing happened!

While shivering violently, feeling helpless and hopeless, I recall hollering out some profound and probably profane requests for help. Still nothing. Exhausted, but not ready to quit trying, I made a few more attempts to reach over the ice and pull myself onto it. When I reached with what could have been my last-ditch effort, my hand came down on something other than ice. I reached out with my other hand and discovered a short but solidly frozen-in tree branch. I believe I shouted a prayerful "Holy shit!" I was now able to grip enough of that branch to pull myself over the surrounding fragile ice. It may not have been as noteworthy or as divine as I had hoped for; however, the placement and discovery of that branch will remain as one of my most sacred moments!

I lay there for a couple of minutes, motionless, exhausted, and shivering with glee. And then, things got even better. I heard my buddies hollering my name as they skated toward the bridge and me. I screamed for them to stay back away from the bridge and wait for me to crawl toward them. They had missed one of my life's greatest breakthrough performances, but they arrived in time for the finale.

After helping me off the ice and sharing some warm, dry clothing, we managed to find a diner nearby. I discovered the pure joy of a cup of hot coffee. Even the smell of coffee had always made me cringe with disgust. Since that night, and to this day, I could die for a cup of coffee. Almost did!

Over the months that followed, I would often stop and think about the two close calls on ice. The conditions that played into my survival then and during previous unexplainable events started a process of wonderment about my existence. I began to wonder if guardian angels actually exist and step in when needed. If so, why? Could it be that these events really are like pieces of a puzzle about some purpose for my life? I had no idea!

5

Double-Trouble Trucking

D riving a large, open-sided truck crammed with cases of bottled beverages is a challenge. Open sides require a constant watch for potholes, a delicate touch accelerating and braking, and a most skillful handling of sharp turns. As a summer driver for a small beverage company in Red Bank, New Jersey, I worked alone delivering over three hundred crates a day to grocery stores, restaurants, and bars along the Jersey shore.

The days were long and the summer heat and humidity miserable. But at the age of seventeen, I could not complain about the conditions or the fifty-six-cents-an-hour pay. The incentive was great to stick with the job, save the earnings for college tuition, and hopefully earn a better salary someday! The summers I spent driving a truck helped me learn a lot about responsibility, patience, and people. I also learned that no matter how hard you work, follow all the rules, and perform consistently at your absolute best, shit happens! The next two stories from my beverage-delivery days are examples of just how fast one can lose control of a situation, one's job, and even one's life.

BRAKE FAILURE

I was halfway through a hot, sticky summer, working one day on a route in Highlands, near Sandy Hook, New Jersey. I was approaching the top of a mile-long, straight, and steep two-lane road that ended in a T-intersection at the bottom of a hill. I made a gentle, slow turn at the top of the hill while admiring the wonderful view of the Atlantic Ocean. My enjoyment of the view, however, was suddenly interrupted when a creepy, uneasy feeling came over me. I had driven this hill many times over the years without a concern of any kind. The importance of good brakes had always been obvious, but I never felt that they could possibly fail.

Having gained some respect for gut feels about any issue, I stepped on the brake pedal as a precaution. It went clear to the floorboards! In total disbelief, I tried again, and again. I hoped that by pumping the brake pedal I could get some brake fluid flowing and get it working. Wrong! I looked straight ahead, noticed that the road was free of traffic, but saw that many cars were parked on both sides. Any thought of slowing the truck by driving it onto someone's front yard was quickly dismissed. The speed of my heavy, open-sided truck full of crates began to increase. I tried to pull up on the hand brake, a marginally functional tool when gaining speed rapidly. Not much help for what was quickly becoming profoundly serious!

I didn't swear much as a teenager, but I do remember a few panicked shouts involving God and some nasty words. Then, I remember a firm request: "What the hell do I do now?!" Ahhh, seconds later, a thought from within, beyond, or wherever. Downshift! Yes, do it; forget what it does to the transmission, I thought. The grinding of gears was a minor concern. I also began to scream: "Get out of the way! *No brakes!*" while leaning out an open window. I was hoping to at least get the attention of people farther down the hill!

I estimate that my speed must have been about forty miles per hour when I was about two-thirds of the way down the hill. People were stepping out onto their porches and from their lawns to marvel at this amazing sight. They were witnessing a swerving-to-slowdown, bottle-spewing, gear-grinding truck with a maniac driver screaming out the window at the top of his lungs: "*Look out!*"

What followed next, I suspect, was part miracle, part luck, and part panic-inspired driving skill. Now, decades later, I still laugh at the memory of simultaneously pumping the floor brake, working the hand brake, shifting to lower gears, beeping the horn, and screaming out the window. Just a few hundred yards from the T-intersection at the bottom of the hill, the truck started to slow down.

To my relief and the amazement of a crowd gathering at the intersection, it looked like the truck might slow down enough to avoid plowing right through the stores at the bottom of the hill. I took as broad and as smooth a turn as I could just short of the sidewalk ahead. The truck tipped just as the front outboard wheel smacked hard against and over the curb. That maneuver kept the truck and me upright and free of injury, stopping just short of the crowd. The whole glorious maneuver and launching of several dozen crates of beverages into the air were a delight to the applauding crowd.

It took quite a while to calm my nerves, my mind, and my heart rate. I then called my boss from a local store (no cellphones then), explained what had happened, and requested help in cleaning up the mess. Help arrived within an hour and included one of the company supervisors. He took care of my transportation needs, the truck, and the mess. I was even given the rest of that day and the next day off from work.

WHEEL LOSS

You have to admit that losing the brakes of a fully loaded, open-sided truck at the top of a long, steep hill is a pretty unlikely event. Fate, however, was not done with me! On my first day back at work, I was presented with a so-called "better" truck already loaded and ready to go.

Several fellow drivers shook my hand and grinned, probably thinking about the brakes on their own trucks. The tickets for each of my deliveries were already in the cab of the truck, so I jumped in and headed out on my route for the day. My day off was just what I needed. I was refreshed and ready for a calm, uneventful day.

My first delivery was at a diner along State Highway 36 near my home in Leonardo. I knew a few of the waitresses well enough at that diner that they would often offer me a free cup of coffee and a doughnut. Things were going great. Well, that is, until I had traveled just a few miles farther down the highway. A strange sound, sort of a rhythmic squeak, seemed to be coming from the engine or maybe one of the front wheels. It continued for a couple of miles as I searched for a good place to pull over and look for the source of the sound.

At a small clearing off the side of the highway, I stopped, got out, and checked the few obvious things that I thought might be causing the noise. Nothing looked or smelled out of the ordinary, so I got back in and continued down the road. The frequency and intensity of the squeaking were clearly tied to the speed of travel, so I slowed down to about forty miles per hour and kept an eye open for a gas station.

The squeak was soon turning into a loud, more continuous screech. I thought about the nightmare (actually, daymare) I had experienced just two days earlier with failed brakes! I quickly tested my brakes and started to slow down, when suddenly the world around me burst into a horrific explosion of sights, sounds, vibrations, and smells.

It is impossible to capture and describe the confusion and panic of that moment; however, I clearly remember the sudden drop of the truck's front right side and the violent thrusting of my body up and down and side to side. In that same instant, I caught a glimpse of the truck's front right wheel flying into the air. The tire, rim and all, hit the shoulder of the highway and rolled at high speed into an empty field.

Within seconds, the truck veered wildly onto the right shoulder with its axle grinding through concrete and gravel, spraying a stream of sparks high into the air. I instinctively tried to steer the truck back onto the highway to prevent it from flipping over. The remaining left wheel caught and dug into the soft shoulder causing a violent shift in direction. The result was both regrettable and unforgettable as wooden crates and bottles went airborne and shattered over a broad swath of the road. The truck did finally come to a stop on the highway, upright but with a severe list to one side. A bent, red-hot axle, finally at rest, had carved a very long and impressive trench in the pavement.

What a spectacle that event must have been for those in oncoming vehicles as they swerved to avoid the truck, airborne crates, and shards of concrete and glass. I sat for a few minutes, wanting to appear calm, cool, and collected as people arrived to see if I was OK. I do not know whether it was trauma left from the no-brakes incident, emotions from this event that had overwhelmed muscles from my waist down, or both. However, with great embarrassment,

I discovered while stepping down from the cab that hopes of calm, cool, and collected were actually more like shaken, shocked, and shapeless! I fell to the ground with legs of rubber and could hardly get up for several minutes. That was partly OK as I hoped no one would notice that my pants were a bit damp as well.

Once on my feet, I knew it was time to call my boss—again. For sure, he'd think I was joking; that is, until I got to the part where I planned to say, "I quit."

A friendly guy who witnessed the event was quite helpful and gave me a lift to a nearby restaurant with a pay phone. Another responsible-looking young man offered to stay at the scene until I got back or the police arrived. My boss was relieved that I was unhurt and that no one else got hurt. He even had a good laugh at the absurdity of a brake failure and the loss of a wheel just two days apart. He then got serious and assured me that he would get me a "new" truck. I was given the rest of the week off with pay, the old truck and street mess were taken care of, and I stayed with the job (and a new truck) for the rest of the summer.

The latest trucking events, along with the other close calls in my life, did spark some lively debates with my friends about destiny, guardian angels, and death. Their concerns over my well-being were sincere, but they usually attributed the outcomes to coincidence and luck. Unexplainable experiences were simply that: unexplainable.

To me those views were totally unacceptable. I had been too close to serious injury or death. Something strange and

6

Snowed In

C hristmas was only a week away. A break from classes, term papers, late-night cramming, and cafeteria food sure sounded good! My third year at Washington & Jefferson College (W&J) was going well, but I missed my family and friends back home. More than anything, I missed Lydia, my sweetheart for the past five years. She was a sophomore at Wagner College and as always, was heavily involved with her truly first and lasting love: music. She had a big concert coming up in a few days at her college, and I was determined to get home in time to catch her performance with the choir.

The drive from college to New Jersey, about four hundred miles, would normally take about eight to nine hours including a couple of short breaks. A friend at W&J, Joe Pacelli, lived in my hometown and needed a ride home for the holidays. It was great to have someone along for the ride, to share stories, reminisce, and help pay for the gas. Little did we know just how tough this trip would be and how it could have been our last!

The weather reports didn't sound good. They were predicting snow sometime within the next twelve to eighteen hours, and we were planning on leaving the next morning. Under normal conditions I'd have plenty of time to get home, shower, and head over to Staten Island for the Christmas concert. We were worried that if we were delayed, we might run into some serious weather along the Pennsylvania Turnpike, so we rushed our packing, fueled the car, and headed for the turnpike. It was mid-afternoon, cold but clear.

Well, weathermen in the 1950s didn't have satellites and sophisticated meteorological stations all over the place like we have today. Damn! We weren't on the turnpike twenty minutes before snowflakes started falling. And they didn't waste any time sticking to the already frozen ground. It was actually fun, for a while; but within another fifteen to twenty minutes we were starting to worry as the flakes got bigger, visibility dropped to a couple of hundred feet, and the tire tracks of the vehicles in front of us were the only real clues that we were still on the road. It was getting darker and windier by the minute.

My traveling companion suggested that we get off the turnpike and take a more southerly route toward West Virginia or Maryland. We could hopefully avoid the heaviest snowfall and head north again as we approached New Jersey. Conditions actually improved for a while as we moved along with the aid of our compass on roads neither of us knew. It wasn't long, however, before the snow and wind became worse than before. So much for a route farther south!

Soon we were unable to see the road or any homes or businesses along the way. We were crawling along at about ten to fifteen miles per hour for only a short time, when we experienced a complete loss of visibility and an abrupt stop. We bundled up, got out of the car, and discovered that we had driven into a huge snowdrift. There were no other cars or buildings in sight. While tempted to set out on foot, we knew it would be foolish to lose sight of our car and a path back to it. The wind and heavy snowfall would have made it impossible to see our tracks within minutes.

We climbed back into the car and sat for a couple of hours, running the engine now and then to keep warm. Worried about a plugged exhaust pipe and the need for fuel the next day, we decided to turn the engine off and wait for help or the snow to stop. We became increasingly cold, sitting and shivering as we admitted how stupid it was to have left without sleeping bags, warmer clothing, and some food and water. I could just hear my father, as he would soon be saying: "Humph, and you are in college!" Well, some lessons simply get learned the hard way!

Time seemed to lose its significance as we gabbed away, the air inside the car getting colder by the minute, until finally, talking less and less, we drifted off into what seemed a relatively painless and almost comfortable sleep. Hours passed.

I was aware of absolutely nothing! No dreams that I remember, no light at the end of a tunnel, no vision of angels. Simply deep, deep unconscious peace, until a faint sound entered my near-conscious state. Soft at first, it became louder and more distinct, shifting between rapid thumps and taps to pauses followed by heavy, single thuds, like somebody kicking the side of a car door. Little did I know that's exactly what it was! Unable to open my eyes, I listened, still unaware of where (or even who) I was. It must have been several minutes before I could move my eyelids, apparently giving encouragement to whoever was banging on my car door and window—the thumps and taps suddenly got louder and faster.

Within a few more minutes, I was able to move my head a little toward the source of the noise, while the image of a rather panicky face and a small light began to appear. As I reclaimed a modest memory of where I was, I soon realized that a man was pointing a flashlight into the car, hollering something, and then pointing with his glove at the little lock post on the door. It had been pushed down, keeping him from opening the door. I could see the post but was unable to move my hand over to it. Once I could reach it, I was unable to squeeze it tight enough to pull it up. I kept working on it and finally pulled it up! Immediately, the guy pulled the door open and started rubbing my arms and legs, while yelling for my buddy to wake up! When he saw that I was able to move a little better and talk, he then went to work on my friend.

I was so relieved when my travel partner started coming around and making strange sounds. I wondered if I too had made such weird groans as I woke from that deep, cold sleep. It was dark, and the wind had piled snow up over the roof of the car. The man who found us, a strong, confident individual, soon revealed a plan that sounded good. He said that he was driving a snowplow and that he would clear the snow from behind our car and attach a chain so he could pull us back onto the road. After that, he would get in front of us and clear a path so we could follow him. He knew the owners of a roadside restaurant/bar about a mile up the road.

The plan worked, and soon we were banging on the door of a bar that must have closed early that day. A man came to the door and was quite surprised to see our new friend and two dreary, shivering characters behind him. After a quick explanation of our dilemma, the owner of the bar invited us to spend the rest of the night there. He gave us some blankets and pillows; and I remember how good it felt on the floor, snuggled up against one of the pool tables.

Ready for a cozy snooze, exhausted, and still shivering, I watched through heavy eyes as the snowplow driver headed for the door. Suddenly, it hit me: How in the hell did that guy find us in the middle of the night during a blizzard?

I watched as the owner of the building walked with the snowplow driver toward an exit. I then realized that I had not thanked the driver for all he had done. I crawled out from the covers and hollered: "Hey, thanks for digging us out of that snowdrift!" The driver simply nodded with a faint "You're welcome." Realizing that this guy had saved our lives, I called out again: "Hey, wait a minute!" He stopped with the door cracked open, ready to leave, when I asked: "How did you know we were in that car? It was buried in snow! It's the middle of the night!" His expression was a combination of anger, confusion, and fatigue. He mumbled something like "Eh, it was nothin'; forget it" and turned to go outside. I rushed toward him and insisted that I at least shake his hand. He reluctantly turned, shook my hand, and said again: "Forget it, man, I simply move snow and you lucked out!"—or words close to that.

After several attempts to get him to come back in for a minute, he finally caved in, telling me that he really did not want to talk about it. "Frankly," he said, "I'm still feeling a bit spooked by the whole damned thing!" I pleaded with the driver. Now, I *really* needed to know the "spooky" facts. He must have known that I deserved some kind of explanation. I was delighted when he finally grabbed a chair and sat down. My college buddy was already sound asleep, and the bar owner was headed back to his own bed. Alone with this crusty, but treasured snowplow driver, I sat down next to him and listened as he blurted out:

"Look man, don't ya think I'm crazy, or something. . . . All I can say is you sure got some kinda friend upstairs." He looked briefly toward the ceiling, and I knew he didn't mean the bar owner, but someone higher up!

He continued to explain how he had been lying in bed, sound asleep, when he was suddenly awakened by a voice or something telling him to get up and start his run. I assumed that a "run" was his normal route for clearing snow. He said that he thought it was a dream, so he turned over and tried to go back to sleep. He thought he was going crazy when that same voice kept coming back, telling him to get up and start his run. He continued, saying that he was really getting spooked with that "dumb-ass voice" in his head that kept on telling him to start his run. He said he was so freaked out that he didn't know what to do, so he finally got up, dressed, and headed out to his snowplow.

After a few deep breaths and several shakes of his head suggesting total disbelief, he continued his story. The weather was nasty, he said, with strong winds and heavy snow making it tough to stay on the road. After about half an hour, he apparently passed a car or two stuck in the snow, some barely on the road, when suddenly that same creepy voice said: "Stop, check that car." He looked around, and off to the side of the road he saw a chrome bumper sticking out of a snowdrift. He said that he ignored the voice, but it came back even stronger saying: "Go back and check that car!"

His explanation so far was really hard to believe. I could understand why he didn't want to share it with me. He went on though, saying that he got out of his cab and walked back to that car covered with snow. After clearing the snow from a window, he looked in and couldn't believe what he saw: "Two punks, asleep in the front seat," as he put it. He said that he must have banged on our doors and windows for at least five minutes. He was ready to go back and get a wrench to bust out a window because the doors were locked, and we were not moving. But then he thought he saw me move a bit, so he just kept banging on the window.

Wow, what a guy! What a story! I remember him telling me as he headed back toward the door that he had never experienced anything like that in his entire life, and he sure hoped he never did again. He left quickly. I never even got his name. I crawled back into my comfy little niche next to the pool table and passed out.

By mid-day, the snow had stopped, and there was a reasonably cleared path down the road. After thanking the bar owner for his hospitality and getting some directions, we headed northeast back toward Pennsylvania. The going was slow and difficult, but we finally made it to New Jersey. Unfortunately, it was too late to make the Christmas concert, but we were alive and well.

This remarkable event that almost ended the lives of two young college kids remains as a frightening though treasured memory. I have shared it numerous times with colleagues, friends, and family members, each time taking away yet another lesson. One lesson, obviously hard to admit, is the need to fully prepare for any journey and to anticipate the challenges that might arise along the way.

As a physics major at W&J and a budding enthusiast at the time for the principles and value of science, I am not surprised that it took years for me to recognize the metaphysical interpretation of that lesson. Science can explain the potential lethal effects of prolonged exposure to extreme cold, while unexplainable, unscientific phenomena may alter the results of an otherwise certain outcome.

The mysterious events presented here and in previous chapters were increasing my awareness that I should seek a balanced perspective involving both scientifically predictable events and mystical experiences. It seemed that the first twenty years of my life included multiple clues about the path I was on and that there could very well be a purpose for that life. Pieces of the puzzle were all around me, but I just couldn't see how they fit together—*at least not yet*.

7

Celebration Gone Bad

E very year it was a tradition to celebrate the election of our new fraternity president by dragging him, clothes and all, into an ice-cold shower. It was my turn, toward the end of my junior year at Washington & Jefferson College, to be honored with such a celebration by my Delta Tau Delta fraternity brothers. The evening involved a vote, a speech by the outgoing president, and a rowdy surge of fellow Delts toward their new president for the grab and cold-water dunk!

With good intentions and excitement, that energetic lunge was just a bit too chaotic, thrusting the podium and me backward and driving my head and shoulders directly into the glass of a huge window. The impact with the window caused an unusually clean horizontal break of the glass a few feet above my head, while the lower portion of the window shattered outward. My memory of the impact and the few seconds that followed was (and still is) like a slow-motion movie—a scene in which all motion, sounds, and emotions of joy and excitement grind along slowly and then accelerate into an explosion of shock, panic, and fear. As I fell backward shattering the lower half of the window, the slab of glass above my head remained in place. I remember looking straight up at a massive, sharp-edged plate of glass still lodged in the window frame.

It was likely only a second or two during which gravity and momentum drove me into a helpless and dangerous position beneath that pane of glass. As I fell backward, that slab of glass began to slip, as a heavy glass guillotine, from its temporary position. Before anyone could have possibly reached me, I felt a strange sensation (a force from beneath me) lifting my head and shoulders up and forward toward my feet. There was a sudden sharp pain behind my right shoulder and the sound of glass shattering all around me. I stood, shocked but stable, watching as my fraternity brothers stopped dead in their tracks, looking as if they had just seen a miracle.

Oddly, no one was close enough to assist with the rapid body shift that seemed to defy gravity. There could be no claim of credit for heroically pulling my body from the path of that sheet of glass. I was sure that someone was responsible for saving me from certain injury or even death, but not one person could take the credit. Everyone in the room that night was so stunned by what they had witnessed that the usual end-of-celebration party was canceled, and everyone retired to their rooms.

I survived the evening with only a minor cut on my shoulder when the heavy slab of glass nicked me on the way down. It was definitely an honor for me to be elected president, but it was even better to have kept my head about it all!

Yes, this is a brief chapter about a brief encounter with a potentially disastrous outcome. Fortunately, the original plan for a night of celebration also had a brief but happy ending. I was shaken to the core, knowing that I had experienced a lifting of my body from harm's way, a shift I could not have created on my own! The effects of that split-second intervention with fate produced a permanent crease in the fabric of my memory that will never fade. I cannot explain how a millisecond of enormous fear can be replaced in an instant with a phenomenal burst of joyous survival! But that is exactly what I felt. I believed that something beyond my world of comprehension had once again saved my life.

The *why* of it all was a mystery. The evidence of repeated survivals and lessons needing to be learned was growing stronger. I continued to search for answers regarding my own spiritual growth, and I felt that I was making progress. I could see that certain events had definitely given me cause to pause and to appreciate the path I was on.

The clues that gave me hope along that path were strong and positive; however, I soon let down my guard and nearly lost my way. The weight of heavy choices involving a career, marriage, and children overpowered the trust I had put in lessons learned and the belief that an all-knowing source beyond this world was leading me toward a purpose for my life.

The following chapter includes a disclosure of the lowest physical, mental, and spiritual depth I have ever experienced. The recovery from such a *lower place* could have only involved the unconditional love of a *higher source*.

8

Challenging God

This chapter involves a time and place in my life when I was at an absolute low—physically, emotionally, and spiritually. The experience turned out to be a profound turning point in my journey of self-discovery. I learned how vulnerable I could be to the weight of dark events, while then discovering the power to recover with help from a source of love and light.

Some of the events and personal choices described in this chapter may be upsetting. If so, I ask for your patience and understanding as I was at a serious low, ready to give up on life. Remembering and writing about this event have been painful for me, serving as an emotional dump of regrets over my behavior at the time. Fortunately, my descent to an all-time depth of despair exposed a path for healing and enlightenment beyond anything I could have imagined.

It was 1971, and I was making efforts to recover from a recent divorce. The decision to end a marriage of nine years was an incredibly painful experience. The need for change, however, was overwhelming; and I needed to distance myself from an unacceptable relationship and a job that was equally unsatisfying. I had just accepted a new position with an environmental company in Santa Monica, California, and moved into a small apartment with no furniture. The change was difficult and lonely but promising because I was meeting and working with new people and building a whole new career.

The first few months in the new job went well, but the reality of a failed marriage with two children created complications and difficulties I could never have anticipated. My attempts to balance responsibility to my new employer and to my children created enormous pressure, both physically and emotionally.

I slipped into bad habits involving poor diet, little exercise, and short, unhealthy periods of sleep. It wasn't long before I became so sick that I had to take several days off from work. I was suffering through the lowest state of mind and body I had ever experienced, reaching total fatigue and despair.

One night, as I lay shivering with cold sweats, terrible stomach pain, and a fever, I actually started to doubt my belief in God. As the hours passed, I became increasingly depressed and was soon convinced that God could not exist! Why would God let me reach this condition when I had put so much effort into my marriage and my new job?

The darkness in the room, within my body, and in my mind became so overwhelming that I started yelling out loud to the God I was increasingly convinced could not exist. I'll spare you the disgusting accusations and swear words I used that night, language that included the worst of the worst expressions I had ever heard used by anyone. It must have been at least ten to fifteen minutes of continuous lewd and offensive shouting as I lay on my back, challenging whatever could possibly be out there claiming to be God.

Desperate with physical and emotional pain throughout my being, exhausted, and with a sore throat from shouting obscenities, I soon reached the absolute bottom of any capacity to further piss off God. I remember making a final attempt to shout (likely a pathetic whimper) my closing challenge to the Great Almighty Fake—a challenge that I knew would be heard by no one. My final challenge: "Hey! You! This is my last and final call for proof that you exist. I've lost all hope." A few more nasty expletives followed, as I recall, along with a most disrespectful "I am done. Give me a sign, anything, even just a clue that you've been listening and that you give a rat's ass about me."

Silence, more silence, and then . . . Holy crap! All hell (or was it heaven?) broke loose! My feet began to shake uncontrollably, as if someone had grabbed them and wanted to get my attention. Before I could even react to the shaking, my legs and hips started to shiver, leading to an all-out lifting of my feet, legs, and butt several inches into the air as they shivered and bounced up and down.

At this point I remember hollering out: "OK, OK, that's enough! I'm sorry, REALLY! I believe, I believe!" But before I could even hope for a response of sympathy or forgiveness for all the stupid, rude swearing I'd put out there, the shaking and twisting extended upward into my chest, shoulders, and arms. I must have looked like a wild sea creature pulled rapidly from great depth and struck with a dozen high-powered Tasers.

And as if the violent shaking wasn't enough, there was a burst of intense light surging upward, over, and through my body. The entire event seemed to take less than ten seconds, and it culminated in what felt like an explosion of golden light from the top of my head. I must have passed out instantly and fell into a deep sleep until morning.

When I awoke, I felt calm, fully rested, strong, and healthy. I recall looking into a mirror and being shocked at just how bad I appeared. I hadn't washed, shaved, combed my hair, or changed my grungy wrinkled clothes for days. Even though I now felt refreshed physically, I had the strangest feeling that I was not in full control of my thoughts and emotions. There was a vague recollection of the anger and frustrations I experienced during the last few days. It took several hours, however, before I could remember anything about my challenges to God, the uncontrolled shaking of my body, and the explosion of light through the top of my head.

Functioning as if I was under a strange but pleasant controlling force, I showered, shaved, and put on some fresh, clean clothes. I didn't know what day it was, and it really didn't matter. Everything simply felt good and right. I had no plan in mind, skipped breakfast, walked out to my car, and drove off toward downtown Santa Monica. I know that I was in control of the car, but something had dulled my need to know where I was going. I was comfortable just enjoying the moment. At times, fragments of thought would drift back on how sick I had been the last few days and how depressed and angry I had been the day before.

The next thing I remember was pulling into a parking lot full of cars, finding a space, getting out of the car, and walking toward a long row of buildings. I walked past a large double door where a welcome sign had been set up on a portable easel. I didn't know it at that moment, but I was standing at the entrance to a church.

I had no knowledge that it was Sunday morning and that a service was underway inside. Without hesitation, I opened the door and found myself at the back of a large room filled with people listening to a woman speaking from a small elevated pulpit at the front of the church. Normally, faced with this situation, I would exit quietly, trying not to disturb any of those in the pews nearest the door.

Not this day. Not with the spell I seemed to be under. No, this magical morning of surprises had me walking straight ahead without hesitation, looking for a space to sit. Finding none, I continued walking all the way to the front of the church, where I saw an empty seat in the front row directly in front of the pastor. With several surprised glances from the congregation, and yet a warm smile from the pastor, I sat down. She never missed a beat with her sermon, and to my amazement, she spoke for at least another ten to fifteen minutes, rarely taking her eyes off me. Her message and the seemingly personal connection with me were exactly what I needed to hear and feel that day.

It was as if an all-knowing source beyond this world was speaking through her, knowing exactly what I had done and experienced the previous night. She spoke of the mysteries in life, the events that are perfectly timed, and how each of these experiences has the potential for profound spiritual growth. I had to fight back tears of heartfelt joy and relief as she spoke of infinite love and acceptance always there for us no matter what we say or do. I found comfort in the suggestions that each soul is here for a purpose, that we always have control to choose or to "program" our own life and to learn from the choices we make.

I knew, as the service ended, that my doubts and ugly challenges of the night before could never offend the *Infinite Source of Love and All That Is*. My connection with self, both body and soul, and with a renewed desire to live and learn gave me courage to deal with the challenges in my life.

This learning experience provided a lasting desire to recognize and better appreciate signs, or steppingstones, along my life journey. There had already been many stones—some avoided, some jumped over, and others tripped on causing a near-fatal fall. All, as it turns out, became reasons for writing this book. My goal is not to help you, the reader, to avoid such stones, but to see and treasure their role in your life. When moved to do so, leave no stone unturned—nuggets of profound insight may be found.

Such was the case for me over the next few years. Within a year I was offered a new and exciting job as manager of an environmental consulting firm. I expanded my field of expertise into studies and experimentation with oil spills and their impacts on ocean-floor communities of plants and animals. These opportunities led to week-long stays in an underwater habitat, Hydro-Lab, and to resulting life-changing enhancements and relationships.

A most significant and rewarding change involved the meeting of a beautiful young woman, Anda, who captured my heart and soul. We married and within a year moved to Alaska. Mysterious, unexplainable events continued to change, challenge, and enhance our path together. Some of those events were so exciting and even life-changing that I've included them in the next few chapters.

9

Moose Encounters

One of my favorite activities while living in Alaska for fifteen years was cross-country skiing on the many wonderful, well-groomed trails in and around Anchorage. My wife and I had been avid downhill skiers before moving to Alaska, but we quickly discovered that cross-country skiing was the in-thing. Having just bought my first pair of cross-country skis and poles, I thought, "Hey, this can't be much different than downhill skiing." Wrong!

Following are three lessons that honed my skiing skills, while confirming that all paths in life, even those in snow, may present unique challenges. More importantly, there seems to be a trend for unexplainable close calls along my own life path—perhaps needed to grab my attention!

LESSON 1

There was a narrow trail through the woods near our home, so I put on my new skis one afternoon and started shuffling my way onto the trail. Within a minute or two I was quickly humbled by the difficulty of achieving a coordinated shift of the skis and poles. The unattached heel of my ski shoes to the skis was so unlike the rigid connection of downhill ski boots. Narrow, improperly waxed skis and longer poles, combined with my own inability to perform an alternating push and glide, resulted in several trips and falls.

Failure was not an option. I struggled for at least fifteen minutes, managing to stumble a good hundred to hundred and fifty yards down the trail. Several dogs barking off in the distance seemed a happy distraction from my humiliation. The barking soon got much louder. I glanced ahead down the trail and could see that there were at least five or six extremely excited dogs running directly toward me on that narrow trail. I realized that the width of the trail and the huge snowbanks between tightly spaced trees along each side offered little room for them to pass by me. That concern became even more frightening when I realized that the lead dog was enormous and had a full rack of antlers.

The Alaskan moose can weigh well over a thousand pounds and reach seven feet in height at the shoulders. That moose could have done some real damage to a dog (or a human!), but the number, size, and howling of the pack had him spooked.

I knew that the few hundred yards between me and that moose could close in a heartbeat—well, perhaps at my heart rate, more like a thousand heartbeats! There was no room to hide in the hard-packed snowdrifts, leaving only one option: turn around and try to make it back to the much wider opening where I had entered the trail.

I quickly discovered that turning around on long, skinny skis on a narrow trail takes practice. To my delight, I somehow managed an inelegant turn and let my body, brain, and adrenaline kick in. After a few clumsy attempts to push and glide, I started to get some coordination between my pole thrusts and rapidly improving leg strides. What took at least fifteen minutes to cover earlier now took only a minute or two, and I was cruising! As I reached open space at the entrance to the trail, I dove to the side, watching as that huge Alaskan moose and his marauding band of barkers flew by just seconds behind me!

I lay there on my stomach for several minutes, gasping with a sweaty face happily buried in crisp, cooling snow. My muscle-cramped legs lay straight back with skis still attached and forming a giant X flat on the ground. I remember my gasps turning to laughter as I joyfully accepted the gift of life and the realization that a moose had just taught me how to cross-country ski.

Lesson 1: Stress, adrenaline, luck, and maybe
an angel or two can do miracles!

LESSON 2

A few years later, I had become an accomplished (well, more confident) cross-country skier. I would normally ski after dinner many nights during our long, dark winters. Many of the trails in Anchorage were lighted and well groomed. One of my favorite trails was beautiful, comfortably hilly, and close to the home we designed and built just a few miles away. The dense forest and deep snow created a perfect habitat for the enjoyment of people, bears, and moose. Unfortunately, all three of these critters find that groomed trails provide the most convenient means of travel.

It was a beautiful, clear night with temperatures well below freezing and lots of devoted skiers out for some fun. I had just completed a challenging steep hill and was about to head down the winding back side when up ahead a group of skiers had gathered along the trail. They were frantically calling out to me that a moose was in the middle of the trail just downslope from them. They wanted me to slow down and join them on the side of the trail until that huge bull moose decided to move. I happily did so.

Within a few minutes, another skier rounded the top of the hill, so we all joined in again shouting out warnings to slow down and wait. To our surprise the skier ignored our warnings and kept on skiing at a good clip down the hill. As our shouting increased in volume and intensity, the intrepid skier suddenly placed his poles over his head and clicked them together loudly three times. At this point he was only about a hundred feet from the moose, and to our amazement the moose suddenly looked up at the skier and quickly moved off the trail. The moose then walked slowly into the woods, the skier flew by with a cocky smile on his face, and we all broke into applause for his accomplishment. No one had ever witnessed such a daring move. I tucked that experience away for possible consideration, hoping that I'd never be tempted to try it.

Well, just two nights later, on the same slope of that favorite trail, guess who was waiting below. Yes, it was another group of skiers screaming warnings of a large bull moose solidly planted in the middle of the trail. I had only a minute to balance the weight of wisdom against my ego-fed excitement for an opportunity to become a hero. I chose to heroically continue my glide toward the crowd and the moose, carefully assessing my distance, until at last it was time for the magic three-click overhead-pole maneuver. With a blend of courage in my head, fear in my heart, and a forcefully achieved confident face for the crowd, I did the mighty three clicks.

I'll never know if it was the same, apparently well-trained moose from the earlier experience or just luck, but that moose looked up at me and walked off the trail into the woods. Whew! I continued on with my now authentic smile of confidence and the applause of an appreciative audience.

Lesson 2: Don't let one great success go to your head!

LESSON 3

My ski adventures on the same trail had been free of moose for a few weeks. It was a typical cold, clear day with the last of the early afternoon twilight enhancing my connection with the beauty and fresh air of Alaska. Life was calm and good; that is, until I approached a long, fairly steep segment of the trail where it became narrow with recently plowed snowdrifts on each side pushed into dense-growth forest.

As I began my decent, I noticed what appeared to be a large, dark figure near the bottom of the hill. About a third of the way down, that figure turned, revealing another fully mature bull moose with exceptionally large antlers. There was no group of skiers nearby with shouts of "Moose on the trail!" I actually stopped to assess the risks of advancing with a forceful three-click effort versus a slow retreat up the hill. After all, there were no witnesses to cheer for success or to notify my next of kin should this moose be in a bad mood.

In keeping with the history of bad risk assessments revealed in other chapters of this book, I decided to give the three-click test a try. I do not know if it was my cautious speed-controlling slide (skis in a V-shape) or the fact that this moose like most animals could sense that I was scared. But when I performed my best clicking of the poles, that moose slowly lifted his head (and rack!), glanced at me for a few seconds, and started walking toward me. *Holy shit!* I thought, as he picked up his speed. I knew that I could not turn and race up the hill to avoid a confrontation and that doing so would confirm his assessment of an easy "take."

It was likely less than ten to fifteen seconds when that beautiful beast was within forty to fifty feet and coming on strong. My only option was to leap into a hopefully deep, loosely packed snowdrift between trees, land face down, cover the back of my head and neck with my gloved hands, and pray.

As I dove into a large drift, the snow was unfortunately packed and hard. I did not sink down deep in the drift as I had hoped. On the way down, I broke one of my bamboo ski poles and jabbed the sharp end of the other pole into my ankle. I faked death the best I could, held my breath as long as possible, and waited for the crushing blow of a hoof. It was eerily quiet. Hoping that the moose had just walked off, I turned ever so slowly and looked up.

Good grief! How can I explain what it is like to look directly into the nostrils of a moose, each nostril the size of a large coffee mug, just inches away? His head hung over me for what seemed like an eternity, sniffing and then snorting the most disgusting damp breath imaginable directly into my face. I tried to hold my breath again and fight off the urge to throw up. I am not sure if it was his breath or my fright that made me want to barf.

I lay there motionless, waiting for a fate I knew I could not control. At one point the moose turned his head slightly, his enormous eye staring into my eyes, probably trying to decide what to do with this helpless human. He didn't move his head or change that probing look into my eyes for what seemed at least a full minute.

Unbelievably, I started to relax. I know it is hard to believe, but I felt as if a comfortable connection of some kind had been established for a brief moment with that majestic animal. I started to feel confident that he was not going to crush my skull. Finally, that huge, amazing animal lifted his head and backed away. I waited for at least ten minutes before I got up and walked, skis on my shoulder, back to my car.

I will never forget the feelings of that encounter with such an enormous animal and the rapid transition from absolute fear of dying to an unexplainable shared connection of respect with a creature that could have crushed my head like a melon. Whether deserved or not, I came away from that experience unharmed and thankful for another opportunity to love and respect animals. I also continued to be in awe of the many times I seem to have been spared from serious injury or death.

Well into my late thirties, I was finally beginning to accept that maybe I do have a mission. Maybe it's about time that I give some serious thought to what it is I'm supposed to do in this life.

Lesson 3: Never try the three-click maneuver again unless you have a foolproof backup plan.

10

Love and Learn

The summer of 1977 in Alaska was nearly over. My wife and I had been living in Anchorage for about two years. Recently hired as the manager of an oil spill response company just two months earlier, I had no idea that my views on life and death would soon be changed forever!

It all started while I was sitting at my desk poring over technical manuals, corporate guidelines, and financial reports. I was fully occupied with the challenges of the new job and a desire to learn all I could about the parent company. Then, out of nowhere, an overwhelming feeling like nothing I had ever felt before swept over me.

The feeling was not so much physical, as it was more like a strong emotional "knowing." I didn't hear a voice. I didn't have a vision. It was as if a message was coming through, but my brain (at least at a conscious level) could not comprehend its meaning. I felt that there was something I was supposed to know and act upon, and yet there was nothing I could see, hear, or even imagine that gave clarity to what I thought I needed to know.

Sitting at my desk, fearing that I was losing my mind, I soon experienced a strong desire, almost an instruction from deep within, to *go home!* As the instruction to go home took on greater intensity and clarity, I suddenly knew that I was not being told to go to my home in Anchorage but to my folks' home in New Jersey.

This knowing was so overwhelming, so urgent, that when I tried to ignore it or push it aside, it would come back even stronger. It was not frightening, nor was it uncomfortable. It was like a friendly possession of my mind.

I started flipping through magazines on my desk and almost immediately found an announcement of an oil spill meeting back on the East Coast in about a month. There were topics of interest and some presentations that could help me run a spill response organization. The logic was there, but I struggled with the thought of calling my new boss for approval to attend a meeting on the East Coast when I had so much to do right there in Anchorage.

The power of the message to get home, however, was so strong that I could not think clearly about anything else. Convinced that there was no other choice, I called my boss. To my delight and relief, he was supportive and without hesitation said that if I felt the need to attend the meeting, I should go. Little did he know just how strongly I felt the need! Little did either of us know just how incredibly significant the results could have been had he said I should postpone any travel for a while.

After that call, I felt embarrassed and a bit disappointed with myself for acting so impulsively. And yet, it was clear to me that I had to follow through with the arrangements to attend the meeting and, of course, stop off and see my parents. It seemed odd to me then, and especially now, that I didn't feel the need to conduct any other business or visit other relatives while in New Jersey.

As travel plans were set in motion that afternoon, I remember asking myself what the heck that was all about. I really wondered if I had experienced some kind of mental breakdown. It was as if something outside myself had, with a gentle yet powerful hand, guided my thoughts and actions—it had set a ball in motion, and I had no idea why!

Over the days and weeks that followed, I nearly forgot about the upcoming meeting and the crazy feelings that led to it. I had not talked with my folks for at least a week or two prior to the "knowing" event, and I didn't feel the need to call about my upcoming trip. After all, they rarely went anywhere, and I would rather surprise them with my visit.

It may also be an opportunity to explore what was going on between my father and me at this time in my life. When I moved from the East Coast to California in the mid-1960s, my dad was disappointed and took it pretty hard—I guess I never knew just how hard! Then, when business opportunities and strong urgings pulled me to Alaska, he really got miffed and decided not to talk to me for nearly two years! We had already experienced a fairly shallow relationship, brought on by years of his judging me and my fearing him. Our connection only worsened when my move to Alaska drove a bigger wedge between us.

The month passed quickly. I flew back east, attended the conference, and soon began to get the same feelings of urgency to *go home*. At the end of the conference, I headed for my hometown of Leonardo, New Jersey. My visit would be limited to only two days because of the workload back in Alaska, so I rushed home as fast as I could to see my folks.

Along the way, I recalled the intensity of the "knowing" I had experienced a few weeks earlier. Though confused about the purpose of my trip, I was not going to question the source or the reason for that deep emotional push to go home. I experienced a growing sense of urgency to see my parents. But in spite of that, I did not feel the need to call them. I knew my folks almost never went out and that regardless of my dad's mood, my mom would be surprised and happy to see me.

As I approached the house, I did wonder what I would do if they were not there. I also wondered if my dad was still disappointed in me for moving away. He was a good man, but he held onto grudges and could not share personal feelings. When I knocked on the door, I remember expecting to hear my dad's voice inside hollering something like: "Edith, would ya get the goddamned door and tell 'em we don't want any!"

It is almost comical to think back on a TV show called *All in the Family* that was quite popular around that time. My father could have played the role of Archie Bunker (in real life, Carroll O'Connor) without any effort and be so comfortably in character. Archie and my dad had hearts of gold, crusted over with scabs and callouses that made it nearly impossible to trust strangers or anyone of different background, color, or opinion. Interestingly, my mother had the same name as Archie's wife: Edith!

Well, to my total surprise, my father opened the door, looked down the steps at me, smiled, and said, "Hello, son, it is good to see you." His appearance at the door, his choice of words, the tone of his voice, and even more, his *eyes*, will stay etched in my memory forever! His eyes were bluer, deeper, and happier than I had *ever* seen them before. The blue was of such clarity and warmth that when he looked at me, I felt a sense of peace and acceptance (of me!), a feeling that had been missing for an awfully long time.

I cannot explain how pleasantly spooked I felt as it seemed that he knew my reason for being there and that he was happy to see me. As I walked through that door, he placed his arm around my shoulder, pulled me in close, and said how glad he was that I had come home. Maybe I'm just a silly old wimp, but my eyes leak every time I think about that brief moment—a time when he and I shared a common space, a kind of unexplainable and pleasant connection.

As we entered the house, my dear, sweet mama, the second oldest of fourteen children and wise beyond her years, soon appeared from the kitchen and happily said, "Alan, what a wonderful surprise! I'm just whipping up your Dad's favorite, pot roast and boiled potatoes."

That afternoon, after a scrumptious early dinner, not a minute was wasted on cleanup and dishes. Hours were spent, to my surprise and delight, recalling past family events, the latest gossip about our neighbors and relatives, and the challenges of getting old. I told them all about Alaska and my new job, and there was never a word of anger, frustration, or discontent from my father. He never grumbled about my living so far away, and he seemed to be at peace with life, me, and himself.

Throughout the day there was no discussion of the strange "knowing" that had come over me nearly a month earlier. Nor did either of my parents mention the extraordinary event (totally unknown to me at that time) that had recently threatened to turn their world upside-down.

As the evening wore on, Mom got tired, apologized, gave me a big hug, and said that she was going to get ready for bed. As she headed for the bedroom, I noticed that my dad was sitting comfortably in his favorite chair, smiling (with an almost mischievous grin), fully awake.

The change in my father, even this surprisingly alert post-dinner condition, was so different from his behavior when I used to live at home. During those years he would settle into "his" chair and rarely make it through a single radio or TV show. Within minutes his head would be bent back fully over the top of his chair, mouth wide open, producing a snore that I was sure the neighbors could hear across the street. We would crack up laughing as a long string of ZZZZs would often be interrupted with a choking gasp/snort/spasm, almost as if he'd sucked in a big bug! Our laughter would never even wake him up.

This night, my father was obviously eager to share some news with me. Now, as soon as my mom left the room, he got up, turned off the TV, came over to the couch where I was sitting, and sat down next to me. He was looking at me in a way that I knew something important was on his mind. He began by saying, "Son, about a month ago . . . I died!"

Holy crap! Dad's really lost it, I thought for an instant. But then, while still confused, my mind raced back and made the connection between what he had just said and the "knowing" I had experienced about a month ago back in Alaska. Before I could react, my dad was already into an explanation of how he was obviously sitting there now, fully alive, but having had an actual experience with death. He assured me that he was not crazy, that I shouldn't worry about his mental health, and that I should just be quiet and listen!

What he told me that night changed my life forever! That grumpy, impatient, resentful, and somewhat bigoted old man I remembered had taken on a glow that showed not only in his eyes but also in the sparkle of his voice and the excitement of the story he was about to tell me. Following are the thoughts, words, and reactions my father shared with me that night and which I carefully wrote down as best I could remember during my flight back to Alaska the very next day.

"Son, we didn't want to worry you about a problem I had last month, so we didn't call you. I had been getting worse, in spite of cutting back on my smoking. The emphysema had been keeping me up hacking most nights and I just felt rotten!"

"Conditions," he said, "kept getting worse until the ole ticker, in spite of the pacemaker, just gave out. Your Mom called for an ambulance and they rushed me to the hospital. I guess I hung on for a while, but while they were trying to get me stabilized, the body just said enough! The next thing I knew, I was floating around up near the ceiling, looking down at my body while the doctors and nurses started running around, hollering about my heart, and moving equipment over near my bed! It was like watching some kind of movie . . . with *me in it!*"

"Now, Alan," he said, "if you think I'm making this up, you're wrong. Please hear me out, cause you ain't heard nothin' yet! While I was watching them work on me, I could clearly hear every word they said, and I could even hear the voices of other people in other rooms nearby. Man, it was pretty confusing at first. I knew I had died! I didn't feel panicky. In fact, it felt rather good. I was totally free of pain, I could see and hear clearly, and I simply wondered what would happen next.

"The answer came pretty fast. I soon passed right up through the ceiling and into what appeared to be a long, dark tunnel. Within seconds, I was moving through the tunnel at what seemed an extremely fast and noisy pace. I soon noticed a small bright light way off in the distance, and I was apparently moving toward it. It didn't take long to get to it; and before I knew it, I was passing out of the tunnel and into a field of brilliant colors—a field with the greenest grass and most beautiful flowers and trees I had ever seen! I had a body, and I stood there with some kind of white gown or robe on while I looked down and saw the blades of grass sticking up between my toes.

"Seems a little nutty at a time like this, but I was really distracted from the whole scene by the feeling of such perfect, soft, green grass beneath my feet and between my toes! In fact, the realization of wonderful sensations at my feet soon shifted to other parts of my being and how good I felt all over! I could breathe with ease, and the air was sweet with the aroma of flowers."

As my dad spoke, I was continually surprised at his choice of words and how warm, sensitive, and expressive he could be. He was a changed man, and I was just beginning to find out why! He went on.

"Alan, it was the most beautiful place I have ever experienced. It was a lot like earth, but the trees and flowers surrounding the spot where I stood seemed more alive, more colorful, and more fragrant than any I had ever seen or smelled before. What really caught my attention was a small stream. It seemed to have living water running gently over and around stones. The water was crystal clear, and the sound it made was like a soft, pleasant, and familiar melody.

"I stood there for several minutes, fully enjoying the sights, sounds, and smells that for too long I had missed on earth. I realized just how much my decisions to smoke, drink, and avoid regular exercise had robbed me of such wonderful sensations. While taking in the beauty of this peaceful place, I remember pausing to check out my body. A pinch and a squeeze here and there revealed that my body was present, but clearly not in the condition I had left it back at the hospital. I felt strong, more alive than ever, and capable of sensing my surroundings as never before.

"As I considered stepping into the stream in front of me, I suddenly felt the presence of my brother, your Uncle Frank. Looking up, I saw Frank standing on the other side of the stream. He appeared to be so healthy and happy. He smiled at me and started to explain where I was and how he was asked to help with my *transition*."

My father reminded me that his brother had died about a year earlier and that it was so exciting to see him. After years of misunderstanding and distance between them, it was only a short time before his brother died that they had settled their differences and became close friends. My father continued.

"Frank was explaining that I had died and that I would have the opportunity to experience these earth-like conditions as I moved over to the *other side*. He explained that the body I was enjoying right now was only temporary, as it would help ease my transition to another spiritual condition.

"It was so good to see him, and I had so many questions. It was odd though because Frank seemed to know my questions before I fully expressed them. In fact, I noticed that I was not only hearing Frank's words; I was sort of feeling them. I was amazed when I realized that we were communicating telepathically—there was no apparent movement of our lips, and yet I could sense very clearly the essence of every word he said."

I remember my dad stopping at about this point, looking soulfully into my eyes, and placing his hand on my knee. He said, "Son, please don't think that this was some kind of dream or that I was under the influence of some drug. My experiences on the other side were actually more real than what seems to be our reality as we sit here right now! Our experiences here on earth, our time here together right now, all feel more like a dream in contrast to the clarity of what I experienced in that special place with Frank!

"While Frank was beginning to explain the nature of my transition, it soon became apparent that directly behind Frank, a brilliant circular light was taking shape, and it was growing in intensity as we spoke.

"Alan, at this point there is no way possible that I can explain the presence or the appearance of that light. The best I can do is to say that as it grew in size and intensity, its purity was without measure, without description, without limit. It was never intimidating, judging, or in any way uncomfortable to my eyes or my very being.

"The light felt like a living *force* or *energy* that seemed to become one with Frank and to communicate along with him in giving me a sense of comfort and acceptance. The highlight of this experience was the manner in which the light and Frank provided answers to my questions as quickly as I could formulate them.

"One of my very first questions involved my worthiness to be there in what surely must be heaven. The light and Frank almost seemed to chuckle a bit as they sensed my fear that I deserved to be in hell. Frank seemed delighted to let me know that there is no hell! He went on to say that there is only a place with conditions very much like this.

"As he continued to explain what it would be like to make the transition, I couldn't help but think about all the things I had done on earth, things that would justify a sure ticket to some place—any place—other than heaven!

"The light, through Frank, acknowledged my concerns and said that I could stop worrying about the judgment of my time on earth. I was told that the only judgment there would ever be would come from me about me. I was told that there is no need for anyone to question the intent of my actions, my decisions, or any other part of the life I left behind.

"At first, I felt relief that only I would have to face the times I had been so selfish, short-sighted, and at times so inconsiderate of others back on earth. But then I began to realize just how painful self-assessment could be. From my new perspective, I could already recognize the hurt and unhappiness I had caused others in so many ways.

"I also became aware of the abuse I had subjected my own body to with alcohol, cigarettes, and poor decisions on diet and exercise. The realization of these choices was so hard to accept, but I also began to sense a feeling of understanding for my choices and how I could do better. The review and assessment of self were painful, but I was beginning to understand how life on earth is an opportunity to learn how to love yourself and others.

"I remember how good it felt to let the light change the way I was seeing myself. It was like a cleansing and removal of painful conditions in my physical being and more importantly, a purging of negative thoughts and feelings I had held onto for so many years.

"Wishing that I could have had such insights back on earth and been kinder to myself and others, I began to wonder why we even live as humans on earth! Without the need of a carefully worded question, the answer was provided quickly from the light through Frank, saying that *the only reason we visit earth is to love and learn!*"

My dad stopped at this point and assured me again that his experience on the other side was more real than any experience he had ever had here on earth. His sincerity, his excitement, and his confidence as I had never witnessed before left me stunned and tearful. I realized that I was receiving a truly profound message from beyond this world and that the message was being gifted to me from a man I had loved and feared in equal measure most of my life. I was witnessing the results of enlightenment that could only come from a direct encounter with a source of absolute love and acceptance.

I realized that the unexplainable knowing to "go home" a month earlier was now explainable. My dad's interrupted transition to the other side had allowed for his return to earth and for us to experience a perfect closure for our time together as father and son.

That evening of renewed connection went on for hours. My dad could not help but go into such detail about the beauty of the rolling green fields and the wonderful sights, sounds, and smells of the trees, flowers, and crystal-clear stream nearby. He was filled with joy beyond description for the time he spent with his brother and the light. He would often come back to the reason given to him for life on earth, that is, to love and learn.

He reminded me, as if it were the only real message he needed to give, that I should never forget the information we shared that evening. He said that I should spend my life learning all that I can about this earth and its endless wonders. And above all, I should learn how to love without expectations, without conditions for that love!

Toward the end of the evening, my dad finally shared what happened as he was about to cross through the stream and join his brother on the other side. His brother raised his arm with an open palm, gesturing for him to stop, saying, "Go back, Charlie, it's not time yet. You need to go back. Don't worry, we'll be together again very soon."

My father told me that he did not want to go back but that he also realized he had something important left to do. Instantly, he found himself traveling back through the dark tunnel he had experienced earlier. This time it was not frightening; and before he knew it, he was back in the hospital hovering above the body he had left behind.

The doctors and nurses appeared to be upset and were busy trying to shock his heart back to life. Within seconds, he remembered a rapid and painful transition back into his body. He was angry and did not want to be back in his fragile body. However, his disappointment over being back was quickly replaced with a sense of peace and acceptance of his old body. He remembered the need to simply love and learn. He was suddenly content and confident that his aching body was simply a fragile, temporary shell for the soul he really was and that he would soon be returning to a condition that was strong, healthy, and free of pain. He was now content to see life with a whole new perspective. He knew that he could handle the events of each day, waiting for what he knew would be a wonderful and exciting return to a place of love and acceptance.

Time passed, and I wonder to this day if my father knew somehow that I would be home so he could tell me about this incredible experience. What an evening that was for me to see my dad so very complete, so much at peace with himself, and so happy!

The next morning, I awoke to my dad saying, "Come on, Son, it's time to go to the airport." I had intended to take a bus, but my dad insisted that he and my mother would enjoy the drive. After breakfast we headed for the airport. Not a word was said about our discussion the night before. As we approached the drop-off for passengers, my dad turned, looked back at me with a "knowing" smile, got out, and walked slowly around to my side of the car.

I said goodbye to my mom and told her how much I loved her. Turning to pick up my suitcase, I was surprised when my dad walked right up and gave me the greatest gift I could have ever hoped for: a firm, strong hug. That warm embrace caught me by surprise as there had been no hugs for many years. He then stepped back, placed his hands on my shoulders, and said ever so slowly, "Son, thank you for coming home. Please don't forget what we talked about last night. I love you!"

There was a final hug and a brief, softly spoken reminder: "I'll be heading back soon, but don't be sad—I'll be in paradise!" Within a few weeks of my return, Mom called and said that Dad had just died. Tear-soaked smiles over his return "Home" were frequent each day as I prepared to fly back to New Jersey. Thanksgiving celebrations were underway across the nation that week, but no one could have been as thankful as I was for the "giving" of closure my dad and I enjoyed that one last day together.

Since that trip back home in 1977, I have come to believe that the knowing I experienced while at work in Alaska was a message from an *all-knowing source beyond this world*. That message to go home took control of my mind and my actions. The result was perfectly timed with the instruction from my father's brother for him to go back as well. There was still something important for him to do. His return from the "other side" brought a desperately needed and most deserved closure for him and for me. Our souls seemed to be guided through a divine intervention to bring clarity, acceptance, and love back into our father/son connection.

Greater even than our remarkable reconnection was the information passed on to me by my father during his nearly completed transition from earth. The explanations regarding one's words and actions on earth, and the post-death assessment of self, gave hope and insight for my typically doubting, science-based frame of mind. The sincerity and conviction of my father and the changes I witnessed in his presence gave me confidence that there was absolute truth in the explanations provided to him by the light.

I accept that his time on the other side, and my own close encounters with death, are not *proof* of what lies beyond this earthly experience. But they have provided profound insights and guidance—important pieces of the puzzle about who we are, why we are here, and what may be next. The explanations given to my dad about loving to learn and learning to love have given me courage and guidance while exploring my own path. I am convinced, more than ever, that the path of every life is part of a divine plan.

11

Premonitions

$\mathbf{M}$ ost people have premonitions. I have had several, and in this chapter I will describe three premonitions that involved mysterious though extremely helpful guidance on safety, my career, and choices for the path I am on. If premonitions can accurately predict events that have not yet happened or provide information that may influence important future decisions, are they not worthy of at least our curiosity?

My own scientific background and comfort with things I can measure and validate with controlled experiments always made me suspicious about premonitions. However, I have selected the following events because I experienced them myself, they proved to be of significant value, and others witnessed the profound importance of each prediction.

I cannot explain why or how such information about the future is possible. Could the existence of premonitions provide at least a modicum of evidence that *something* beyond human comprehension exists? Could unexplainable events challenge our understanding of logic, coincidence, and luck?

There are those who feel that when we die, the brain and all its contents die as well. They feel that the idea of the mind, our consciousness, and/or a soul surviving the death of a brain is ludicrous.

Premonitions, along with many fascinating phenomena involving extrasensory perception, have been studied and documented throughout the world. All of these studies and personal experiences, including my own, are unlikely to change the belief of those who feel that consciousness dies along with the brain. I have never felt the need to prove otherwise. I am comfortable with the reality that *whatever is, is!* I nor anyone else can ever change that.

And so, I offer the following premonitions as simply light reads—hopefully, fascinating accounts causing one to pause and ask why. Do premonitions, unexplainable experiences, and enough life-changing events provide *clues* to *something* beyond the world we know?

PREMONITION 1, THE BIG MOVE

Prior to our move to Alaska in 1975, I was based in Los Angeles, California. At times I was given temporary work assignments in Anchorage; however, those trips had always been rushed, leaving no time for me to get out of the office. Such short visits finally became unacceptable—I rebelled and announced that I was taking a day off. I rented a car and drove down the Seward Highway, the only road south out of town. It was fall, and the mountains were exploding with brilliant colors of red, yellow, green, and gold. The air was cool, crisp, and clean; and the sky was baby blue with scattered, huge, white cumulus clouds. I couldn't have picked a better day to get away and enjoy Alaska.

Just a few miles out of town, heading toward Turnagain Arm, a wide, beautiful tributary of Cook Inlet, I was suddenly overcome by a strong physical and emotional sensation. I slowed down and pulled off on the side of the road. My heart was beating faster, and it felt as if a warm, tingling fluid was surging through my body. I was worried for a few seconds that I was having a heart attack, but fear disappeared in an instant and was replaced with a pleasant, comforting sensation throughout my body and mind. My eyes filled with tears, and I broke down into an odd joyous cry. There was no way I could drive. I turned off the engine and sat quietly for several minutes.

Confused, curious, and comfortable was I, enjoying what seemed like a euphoric state of body and mind. This blissful condition, the autumn colors, and the dramatic view of Turnagain Arm's shorelines left me in no hurry to move on.

I recall a feeling as I sat there, like the "knowings" I've described in previous chapters. A "knowing" to me has been the receipt of a message in the form of words unspoken, of information provided without sound from what seems a source of pure wisdom and knowledge. The message this time was: "This will soon be your home."

Knowing better from experience, I did not reject or doubt this idea. I sat and let it fill my mind with related issues. How could this be! How would my wife Anda feel about this? Could we find full-time jobs here? Should I start to consider a move? There were so many questions in my mind.

The message that this would soon be my home was so clear that I just accepted it as truth and decided to continue my first full afternoon alone in Alaska. I explored small towns, trails along streams feeding into Turnagain Arm, and Portage Glacier near the end of the arm about fifty miles from Anchorage. I began to feel a special connection with the mountains and streams, the phenomenal colors of the changing leaves, and one of the most amazing sunsets I'd ever seen.

What a day! Even the timing of my return to Anchorage was perfect, as I had accepted an invitation for dinner with the parents of an exceptionally good friend. I had never met my friend's parents. This would be my first meeting away from the office with locals—I was especially eager to hear more about life in Alaska.

When I arrived at their home and knocked on the door, I was greeted by the mother of the family. As she opened the door, I was about to introduce myself when she let out a fairly loud and excited comment: "Wow! You've had quite a day, haven't you!"

Surprised by the greeting, I barely got out my name before there was a warm hug and a "Hello, Alan, come on in. It is great to finally meet you."

The evening, the dinner, and the stories shared were fantastic. I felt so welcomed and appreciated for coming by. After a short time, I felt comfortable enough to ask about the unusual greeting at the door. The answer came quickly, accompanied by a mischievous smile: "I am able to sense conditions and circumstances affecting others."

Satisfied with her answer, I then shared the details of my knowing and how it seemed to be a strong premonition of how Alaska would soon be my home. I was told that a message of that kind needs no action on my part—events and opportunities for change will take place naturally. Little did I know just how right she was. The lady of the house radiated a warmth and depth of understanding about my life and hopes for the future. It was a remarkable evening!

I returned to California a few days later and shared my story of a premonition to move to Alaska with Anda. We had been married only about a year! She laughed out loud and made it clear that a move to Alaska would be crazy! Her love of the sun, the beaches, and her career as a corporate librarian with the company that employed both of us was simply perfect—we should not change a thing! I smiled and thought, "Hmm, we'll see."

Well, as you might imagine, within days the Anchorage office called and asked if I would consider coming back to Alaska. They needed me for about a month to help wrap up an important project. To my delight, they also asked if my wife could come up as well to help organize their library and various data-storage systems. The request just blew my mind! I was baffled by the events of the previous week, the message about Alaska becoming my home, and the mysterious support of my friend's mother.

My wife's initial reaction was one of suspicion that I had planned the whole thing. There was also doubt that she could handle a month in Alaska with winter just around the corner. After considerable debate, she finally agreed, and off we went.

The month flew by. The work was satisfying, and we really enjoyed the small-town pace of life. I guess it should not have been a surprise when, toward the end of our tour, the manager of the Anchorage office pleaded with us to extend our stay. Heck, why not? Even Anda, my sun-worshipping beach babe, thought it might be interesting to see what an Alaska winter might be like. After all, some of our best dates involved downhill skiing—a few winter months in Anchorage could be fun!

To spare you the details of a long story, I'll conclude this tale with the fact that fifteen times, Anda said, "Well, maybe just one more year." Those were some of the best, most rewarding, and exciting years of our marriage.

Building a home in the mountains, establishing a rewarding career, and adding two fantastic boys to our family kept us challenged and happy beyond measure for fifteen years.

When we moved south to the Seattle area in 1990, we were ready for another major life-shift. We had confirmed the premonition that Alaska "will soon be your home." Based in Woodinville, Washington, I continued to work as a consultant for another twenty-five years. Much of that time involved projects all over the state of Alaska including most of its villages. That great state and its people will always feel like home.

PREMONITION 2, VAPORS

I share this premonition because it involves a visual message that appeared twice, possibly preventing a serious accident. The first image came to me as I awoke one morning in the home we had built in Anchorage. With eyes still closed, surfacing from a deep sleep, I saw an image of our water heater resting securely with wall straps on a small wooden bench in our garage. The bench was well built to support the heater's heavy water tank about a foot off the floor. The image in my mind was crystal clear, showing a can of paint thinner sitting on the wooden bench just a few inches from the base of the tank. There was no question that the can of thinner in the image was one I owned. I could read its label and a note I had written on the side of the can months earlier.

As I studied the image, I noticed that the screw-on cap for the can had been removed and placed on the bench just a few inches away. The video-like image also showed vapors flowing from the can and down its side to the bench. The danger of such volatile vapors near the pilot light of the water heater was disturbing. However, as I opened my eyes and realized I'd been dreaming, I was relieved that what I had seen was not real. That comfort, however, started to slip away as I thought of other strange and unexplainable events in my life. The more I thought about the vapors in that image, the more it disturbed me.

I jumped out of bed and ran down to the garage to inspect the bench with our water heater. Phew! There was no can of paint thinner with vapors spilling over the side. Now I only needed to explain to my wife why I had gotten up so quickly and run downstairs. I described the image to her and apologized for my overreaction. The world was normal again, but as I drove to work that morning, the clarity of that frightening vision continued to haunt me. It was unlike the visions one might experience during a dream.

Once I was at work, the decisions and activities of the day kept me from thinking about the open can of paint thinner. Unfortunately, I was so busy that I completely forgot that our teenaged daughter and her boyfriend had offered to come over and paint our porch that day!

After wrapping up some paperwork and phone calls, I headed home for dinner. As I approached our house, I hit the remote button to open the garage doors and parked inside. I closed the doors and headed up stairs. Near the top of the stairway, I suddenly stopped as everything around me started to fade from view. Everything, that is, except a clear image right in front of me of that can of paint thinner, exactly as it had appeared to me in bed that morning.

I turned immediately and headed back down the stairs to the garage. When I got to the water heater, I could hardly believe my eyes. There it was, the can with cap removed exactly as it had appeared in both the morning and evening images. I could see the subtle refraction of light as it passed through the heavier-than-air vapors drifting from the open can onto and over the edges of the bench. Had those flammable vapors been moved by air currents into the pilot light just inches away, they could have ignited the bench. As the bench burned, the can could have shifted and spilled its contents over a much larger area.

I replaced the cap on the can and moved it carefully to a safe location. Returning to the stairway, I could not believe that I had seen that same image again, fully awake, in the middle of the day. I was confused but happy for the way things turned out. The discussions during and after dinner that evening, especially with our daughter and her boyfriend, included genuine expressions of appreciation for their painting our porch. However, there was also firm instruction on the proper handling of flammable liquids and their vapors!

The mysteries surrounding premonitions and how events can be revealed before they happen continue to boggle my brain and capture my curiosity. I've learned to take strong gut feelings, persistent thought-like messages, and visions seriously. Such experiences may actually be forewarnings that could save time, money, and reputations. Some might even prevent injury or death. The next premonition, had it been respected as such, could have helped prevent such unfortunate results.

PREMONITION 3, SPILL WARNING

This premonition is one that I experienced when I was fifty years old and living in Anchorage. This is the first time I've ever documented the details of this premonition. I am comfortable, at last, disclosing this event because it has now been over thirty years since it happened. I will avoid mentioning the names of people and organizations (other than those that may be obvious) that could be offended or at least embarrassed by some of the events disclosed.

The experience, as with the previous premonition, involved a detailed vision while transitioning from a deep sleep to a fully awakened state. It happened during the fall of 1988, about six months before the *Exxon Valdez* oil tanker spilled about eleven million gallons of crude oil into Alaska's Prince William Sound. That spill, on March 24, 1989, was the worst oil spill in U.S. history until the Deepwater Horizon spill in the Gulf of Mexico in March of 2010.

For about a month before my premonition, I had been consulting with the organization operating the eight-hundred-mile-long Trans-Alaska Pipeline built to move crude oil from Prudhoe Bay in northern Alaska to the shipping terminal in the southern Alaska port of

Valdez. I had already been working as an oil spill specialist for twenty years and was asked to design an oil spill scenario for use during upcoming field exercises.

The organization wanted to use a realistic medium-sized spill of crude oil from one of its tankers onto open water near or just outside the Port of Valdez. Timing, I was told, was important, and they wanted me to get started right away. With hindsight, it is ironic that I was told to go sleep on it and come up with a good plan. Little did they or I have any idea just how well I'd actually sleep on it!

Within a few days I had an amazingly detailed image appear as I was awakening one morning. The image was clear and in color, showing a tanker hard aground with crude oil surfacing around it. Oil had already spread over a large area, suggesting a major spill. I was familiar with the shorelines of Prince William Sound and noticed that the grounding was near Bligh Reef, just west of Bligh Island. The clarity of the image, the location of the grounding, and a gnawing sense of real potential for such a spill left me confused and uncomfortable—so much so that I thought long and hard about sharing the premonition with anyone.

I researched the location presented to me and concluded that while the water depths could cause a grounding, the location seemed too far off the designated tanker traffic lanes. Still, it seemed a good idea to suggest a tanker grounding scenario to the company that had asked me to develop a hypothetical spill incident for training purposes. I did so right away, suggesting a major release of oil, perhaps on the order of a hundred thousand barrels. I knew I might risk ridicule or at least some teasing if I shared my vision of a grounding at Bligh Reef, but I did so anyway. The results were not surprising.

It was suggested that a spill of that magnitude at that location was unrealistic. One individual even made the comment that a ship captain would have to be drunk to put his ship on that reef. I had to agree, but I suggested that we at least consider a significant spill incident in open waters of the sound. I was told to go back to the drawing board and come up with something much farther north and closer to the response staging areas in the Port of Valdez. It was also suggested that the spill simply involve a single tank and a few thousand barrels. Discouraged but not defeated, I left the meeting knowing that I needed to push for a more challenging spill scenario farther from the port.

Over the next couple of months, I was told that my new scenario suggestions were still just a bit too ambitious. Planning sessions were delayed several times, and proposed field training dates were turned down because of the upcoming Thanksgiving and Christmas holidays.

The premonition-like warning of a major tanker grounding continued to haunt me, and I tried to set up meetings in January to get things rolling. By mid-February, I was so frustrated by the excuses for a delay of spill-drill planning sessions that I nearly gave up. I began to think that maybe what I thought could be a premonition was just a visually enhanced dream. Maybe all the energy I was putting into the scenario design effort simply produced a nightmare!

But at about 2 a.m. on March 24, 1989, I got a phone call from the guy who had criticized my "unrealistic" grounded-tanker scenario just six months earlier. With an almost apologetic tone and a touch of humility, he said, "Alan, I'm sorry to call you at this hour; however, we have a tanker aground in Prince William Sound and . . ." My laughter interrupted the exchange as I blurted out: "Very funny, very funny. I never thought you'd call me in the middle of the night to make fun of my scenario!" After a long pause, he squeaked out: "Al, we really have a serious problem. The *Exxon Valdez* is hard aground on Bligh Reef and leaking badly." He told me to be at the Anchorage airport by 5 a.m. A chartered plane would be there ready to take me and members of their response team to Valdez.

The months that followed made headlines around the world and cost Exxon billions of dollars. That one spill changed the philosophy, regulations, technology, and public response to oil spills forever. I mentioned at the end of "Premonition 2, Vapors," that some forewarnings can save time, money, reputations, and even injury or death. These impacts and so many more did result from the *Exxon Valdez* spill.

I know that a serious all-out effort to plan for and carry out training based on my initial recommendations would probably not have prevented the spill. I can't help believing, however, that a timely, robust drill involving a major spill well outside the Port of Valdez could have revealed significant shortcomings. Such a drill could have helped identify the amount, type, and availability of equipment needed; the number of trained personnel required; and the logistics to support an ongoing remote operation. It is conceivable that the severity of the spill's impacts on people and the environment might have been reduced.

CONCLUDING THOUGHT

The recognition of premonitions and the assessment of their value are difficult. They may only involve a feeling that someone is about to call, and then they do. Some may be experienced as gut feelings about someone or some important decision, and others may include strong knowings or even visions that capture and control your mind and will not let go.

The premonitions described in this chapter are not offered as proof of anything. For me they are simply non-science-based clues that I need to consider as I review the path I've been on in this life. They remind me that it is often the unexpected and mysterious events that contain subtle though profound messages for our spiritual growth.

12

Connections

S ome of my favorite connections with people, often with total strangers, have involved sharing love and respect without a word spoken. Even if there had been an opportunity to speak to each other, neither of us would have understood the language of the other.

Why do I share a few examples of such encounters in a book about clues that can light our way? I do because such brief connections have often enhanced my appreciation for the fact that we are all on a similar path, one of self-discovery and learning the purpose for being here.

I've witnessed how the love and respect for others can be found in the strangest places, under the strangest conditions, with the strangest of strangers. I am sharing only four of many such encounters during my travels. Each experience has been a treasured memory reminding me of the good in others and of the trust to release that same good within myself.

My favorite encounters are those that show just how strongly we are all connected, as if part of a single grand plan to discover each other.

CONNECTION 1, JAPAN

In 1975 I'd been working with a team of students from Tokai University in Japan and an environmental research firm based in the United States. Our mission was to investigate the fate and effects of heavy fuel oil spilled from a ruptured storage tank at Mitsubishi Oil's Mizushima refinery along the Seto Inland Sea of Japan. We had been diving at many locations where some of the heaviest concentrations from the fifty-thousand-barrel spill had entered the sea. Much of the oil had sunk to the seabed and was impacting important bottom-dwelling communities of plants and animals.

Most of the members of our team could not speak English. However, under water that didn't matter as we used hand gestures to communicate. Fortunately, one member did speak English fairly well, and he was able to coordinate our travel plans, daily objectives, and observations. It was a wonderful opportunity to learn about the Japanese culture and the respect of Japan's people for each other and their environment. One such lesson of that respect and its extension to visitors of their country was a highlight I'll never forget.

We had completed a set of dives at a remote island and decided to stop for lunch. These breaks were always so enjoyable, not only for the rest, but for the amazing food my Japanese diving team would provide. While they were setting up our temporary break site with driftwood for seats and a small fire, I decided to go for a short walk along the beach. The weather was warm and clear, and the beach was free of any oil from the spill. The only oil we saw in this region was on the seabed in the form of tar balls mixed with bottom sediment and seaweed.

There were no swimmers and very few people walking the beach. Farther down the beach, a lone person crouched down with a large sack. Out of curiosity, I slowly walked toward the individual, soon realizing that it was a Japanese woman digging for clams with gloved hands and a small tool. Not wanting to disturb her, I was careful not to get too close or to stare at her. Out of the corner of my eye, I could see that she was highly skilled, kneeling quietly and studying the sand nearby. Every twenty to thirty seconds she would dig down quickly and pull up a clam. Her sack appeared to be about half full.

Facing away from her (attempting to be respectful), I knelt down and tried to see if I could detect any signs of clams. After several minutes, I thought I had seen some movement and quickly dug into the sand with my bare hands. After several failed attempts to find a clam, I glanced back toward the woman, catching her as she turned back quickly to her own successful efforts. I was sure I had caught a faint smile as she looked away.

After about ten minutes of total frustration and continued aggressive clam hunting, I stood up empty-handed and humbled by the little old lady with a nearly full sack! During my failed mission, I noticed every once in a while that the skilled clamdigger actually retrieved a clam with only her bare hands. I suspect that it was a courteous gesture of encouragement for me not to give up. As I turned to head back to our lunch site, I caught a glimpse of a tight-lipped smile on a sad face with lowered eyebrows. Ahh, the universal expression that says: "Don't be distraught. At least you tried!"

As I approached the group that was about ready to eat, I didn't need to understand Japanese to detect light, sarcastic wisecracks and giggles about my unusual passion for burrowing in sand. Fortunately, our attention soon shifted to the approach of my unwitting clam instructor trudging slowly through the sand with her sack of clams in hand. When she reached us, she bowed her head toward me with such grace and a gentle grin while reaching out with that heavy sack of clams. I stood dumbfounded and wishing for some way to communicate my appreciation. I didn't want to offend her, nor did I want to take food that would likely help feed her family.

Recognizing my predicament, the bilingual member of our team rushed to my rescue and explained my inability to speak Japanese. She responded with several polite gestures toward the team and then toward me, spoke briefly, set the sack of clams near me, and backed away with a prolonged bow. It is hard to explain the depth to which a moment of genuine caring from a total stranger can lift one's spirit. There was an indescribable connection that I hope she felt as well. My emotions surfaced without warning, making it nearly impossible for me to keep my eyes from leaking a bit.

My translator, sensing the significant silence of the moment, broke in with an explanation for me of just how unique the encounter was between the woman and our team. He said that they were a bit shocked to see her approaching our gathering, unaccompanied by a man and coming as close as she did. When she reached out with her gift for me and her expression of appreciation for my efforts, they understood and thanked her for her generosity.

Clues involving the connection we share with other people are often missed or undervalued. I am always thankful for these close encounters, no matter how brief or with whom they occur. They often remind me that even during sad or lonely times, there may be special, seemingly magical communications between souls.

CONNECTION 2, MALTA

In 1979 I was attending an international oil spill conference in Malta, an archipelago in the Mediterranean Sea between Sicily and the coast of North Africa. The conference was a huge success, revealing the latest technology for oil spill prevention and control. Even more exciting for me was the discovery that Malta is a nation with numerous historic sites reachable by bus, boat, or rental car. There are fortresses, temples, and a subterranean complex of halls and burial chambers dating back thousands of years B.C.

It was no surprise to my wife when I called her at the end of the conference and suggested that I take a few extra days before returning home. I just could not leave Malta without visiting the countryside, museums, and as many historic sites as possible.

I started out on my tour of the main island by bus. I was delighted to learn that many of the local people riding the bus spoke both Maltese and English. The bus driver overheard me talking with a couple about my attendance at the spill conference and that I was from the United States. His English was fairly good, and he had lots of questions about my home in Alaska, my travels to other countries, and other aspects of my life. I stayed on the bus for hours, captivated by the sites and the stories of so many attempts to rule that small nation.

The bus driver was a history buff and urged me to spend part of the next day with him again. He offered to let me ride for free, saying that he could drop me off for one- to two-hour stays at special visitor stations, museums, and other places, and then pick me up for the next area of interest. He did just that, and so successfully that I spent the next two days with him as my tour guide and almost private bus driver. He introduced me to nearly every passenger that got on the bus and almost always had a brief story about them and their family.

Toward the end of my last day touring the island, the bus driver asked if I would enjoy meeting a local family who were friends of his family. He said that they would be so happy to entertain someone from the States and to introduce me to delicious Maltese food. Of course, I said yes, and to my surprise he had already set up a tentative meeting at their home for dinner that evening. He warned me that most of the family spoke no English but that the father of the home could be of some help with communications. I felt safe and secure that I was not being set up for a Maltese kidnapping, so I wrote down the address and time.

The home was within walking distance from my hotel. It was a narrow three-story building squashed between and attached to other similar homes. When I arrived, I was greeted by the mother and father, a grandparent, and several children. I remember feeling at ease, even though English was not spoken.

A world map was laid out so that I could show where I had been raised, educated, and lived. Using some photos I had with me, I showed them pictures of my family and Alaska. It was fun drawing pictures of various types of oil spills, methods of cleanup, and how my work involved most major oil companies. The dinner was a delicious local cuisine of size and presentation worthy of a major holiday.

With the help of the father and his limited English, I learned about their heritage, education, age, employment, and other facts of their lives. Using familiar terms, hand gestures, facial expressions, hand-drawings, photos, and other methods, we learned so much about each other. Even the children stayed through most of the discussions after dinner. They listened mostly, spoke some very limited English, and showed off their hobbies and treasured items. Every once in a while, I'd stop and realize just how comfortable I felt in their presence and how it seemed that we were communicating valued feelings—few words were needed.

Flying home the next day, I felt as if I had been with family. We had enjoyed three to four hours eating, drinking, and sharing experiences about our families and homes thousands of miles apart. We all knew that the pleasures of the evening were temporary and memories would fade, that we would likely never see each other again, but that the connection desired between souls is strong and lasting. As with so many of my travels around the globe, the greatest rewards have always involved the connections made between open hearts and caring souls.

Connection 3, Greenland

A polar bear tried to mate with a fifty-thousand-gallon bladder tank—at least that was one of the favorite rumors at the time. The bear's intentions will never be known, but there was strong evidence that mighty claws tore a hole in one of seven large storage bladders containing Jet-A fuel. It was mid-winter 1987 with over seven feet of snow surrounding the bladders within a bermed area at Constable Pynt in Jameson Land, East Greenland. I made four trips to the spill site to help a major oil company with recovery of the spilled fuel.

My involvement spanned all four seasons, with a wide range of rapidly changing weather conditions. It was necessary to be creative while constantly modifying spill-recovery tactics. I was fortunate to have a highly motivated team of Greenlandic Natives from a local community to help with the spill control efforts. They were all hard workers but had no experience cleaning up oil spills. The challenge was further complicated by the fact that no one on my field response team spoke English! Back at the base station there was a translator who would help with overall plans and objectives each evening.

My first visit to the spill site was in mid-winter and went well. The team and I could function effectively with hand gestures, drawings in the snow, and practice with key words like "Need break!", "Lunch time!", "Stop!", and "Help!"

The goals for each day were simple and involved digging trenches through deep snow to the fuel-saturated snow layer about a foot in height next to the berm liner. The spilled oil would drain slowly into the trenches, where it could be removed with suction pumps. I would normally stay on-site for two to three weeks and then head back home for a couple of months.

The work accomplished by the field crew during my first absence was impressive. They had identified the region of saturated snow and completed nearly all of the trenches needed to access the spilled fuel. An early spring melt had begun, and the trenches were now filling with meltwater as well as fuel.

Near the end of my second visit, the trenches had filled with water five to six feet deep with one to two inches of fuel floating on top. Spilled-oil recovery had shifted to skimming with state-of-the-art rope-mop skimming systems that picked up mostly oil and very little water. The greatest risk during these operations involved the use of wooden planks placed across the trenches to get from one side to the other.

A remarkably chilling event took place when I was working at the spill site with just one man from our Native crew. Thankfully, he was the tallest and strongest man on the team. Unfortunately, he was also the heaviest team member. We had just positioned a skimmer in a trench about five feet wide and full of water with a thick layer of fuel oil on the surface. One of our standard wooden planks had been set securely in place across the trench. And, while checking the position of a skimmer, I had stopped on the plank about halfway across the trench. All was going well until my Native coworker of impressive size and weight decided to step out onto the plank as well. There was no time to holler "Stop!" in any language!

Within seconds we both heard the most frightening and unwanted sound of breaking wood! Our combined weight was just too much for that board, and in we went. Our panicky, bilingual duet of swear words was quickly silenced as we splashed through the oil layer to the frigid waters below. Our heavy winter clothing was saturated immediately. For me, however, the penetrating cold water was forgotten and ignored in an instant as I swallowed and perhaps inhaled some fuel oil. Surfacing, I could barely take a breath, let alone yell out, with the choking irritation of fuel in my throat. The oil had also splashed into my eyes, and the pain was so unbearable I couldn't open them.

Fortunately, I could stand on my toes, lips barely above the surface, as I managed a squinted, blurred view of my surroundings. My first image was the back of my soggy co-plank-walker, bounding like a whale from the sea, up and over the bank of snow surrounding the trench. I watched with shock and horror as he struggled to his feet and ran at top speed away from the trench and me!

For a minute or two, but seeming much longer, I attempted several great Greenlandic leaps from the trench. Each attempt was a total failure since the slightest bending of my knees to jump put my face under oil and water again. The minimal reach of my arms also eliminated any chance of pulling myself up and over the slippery snowbank surrounding the trench.

I remember a vague wisp of a thought (fearful then, almost funny now) of the irony that I, an oil spill specialist, might drown in a pool of water and oil. Thoughts and motion of any kind soon slowed to an unexpected, almost comfortable state of mind and body. I was aware of the serious life-threatening situation I was in; however, I also felt a calming presence and unexplainable sense that all would be OK.

That moment of both physical discomfort and a peculiar sense of trust was joyfully interrupted by the sight and sounds of my arctic hero returning to save my butt. I didn't care where he had gone. I could not care less about the words he was shouting. I could read his panicked, remorseful facial expression. But most importantly, I marveled at the ease with which he reached down with one hand, grabbed my outstretched arm, and pulled me out of the trench. I got the grandest bear-hug of my life from this huge, soggy, fuel-stinking giant of a man. He then helped me stumble back to the truck, placed me in the passenger seat, and drove like a crazed father-to-be back to base camp.

Hot showers, warm dry clothing, and a good meal helped our bodies, but our brains had to sustain the endless jokes and cruel nicknames gleefully awarded the two of us. The translator told me in private that my fellow trench-diver felt enormous grief and regret for his thoughtless and untimely walking of the plank and for his initial fearful exit toward the truck. I forgave him and thanked him for coming back to pull me from the trench. The special relationship we discovered, the facial expressions of respect and caring, and the exchange of gifts during my last visit to Greenland speak more to me in treasured memory than any words we could have ever shared.

I often wonder if the calming comfort I felt in that trench and during other near-life-ending experiences is tied to a unique pre-life plan that I was destined to discover. Or could it be, as some claim, that a force or guardian spirit watches over us and steps in as necessary to keep us alive until we've learned enough? I suspect that many events both good and bad serve as clues for learning along each person's path. If that is true, then the number of learnings I've described in this book suggest that as a man in his eighties, I must be a very slow learner!

CONNECTION 4, KOREA

In 1995 I traveled to South Korea as a technical advisor for the International Tanker Owners Pollution Federation Limited based in London, England. The crude-oil tanker *Sea Prince* had grounded on a submerged rock off Sori Island, spilling approximately five thousand tons of oil. By the time I arrived, the oil had already spread and impacted the nearby coastal region. There was also a potential for bad weather and a shift of the tanker causing additional spillage. I was asked to evaluate the risks and benefits of conducting a controlled burn of any resulting spillage. There were large, protected coves nearby where oil could have been contained and burned. Such burning would have likely eliminated large quantities of oil quickly, thereby minimizing the spread of oil and damage to the environment.

Fortunately, weather conditions allowed for safe removal of oil from the tanker without additional spillage. My expertise with the controlled burning of oil on water was not needed; however, before I left the area, I had an afternoon to explore the local community. I set out on foot toward a heavily wooded hill near my hotel.

As I approached the base of the hill, there was a clearing with some large rocks set back off the main road. Two narrow dirt trails led from the clearing in nearly opposite directions. Each trail appeared to curve back toward the top of the hill, so I had no idea which one to take.

While standing and contemplating my next move, I noticed a small elderly woman wearing lightweight summer clothing and sitting on a rock near one of the trails. As I approached the clearing, the woman had her eyes closed as if meditating but soon cast a sleepy glance my way. Trying to be respectful of her quiet time, I paused to examine the two trail options. And to my surprise, the lady rose slowly from the rock and pointed toward the trail entrance farthest from us. She was quite aware of this foreigner's need for guidance.

Feeling certain that English might not be appropriate, I offered a smile of appreciation and the slightest bow of my head to respect her kind gesture. I then set off on the trail she had suggested, as she returned to her rock for continued peace and quiet.

The trail went for about a hundred yards, with several small turns as it led up the hill. It was a gentle slope at first but became steeper as it approached another clearing. Curiously, there was another woman sitting on a rock resting at the clearing. She sure looked like the lady I had seen at the beginning of the trail. Also curious was the appearance of another trail, giving two options to continue up the hill.

As I got closer to the second woman on a rock, I was pretty sure that she was the same Korean lady from below. My suspicion was confirmed as I got a closer look at her face, smiling just a bit more than before. And without hesitation, she pointed quickly to the trail located just behind her position. I smiled along with a fake frown back at her as I began my trek up the trail of her choosing. I stopped at the first turn to look back and confirm that she was still sitting where I saw her last. I then broke into a light jog, figuring that if there was another clearing up ahead, I'd surely beat that little elderly Korean lady to it.

What? How could this be? There was another clearing, and there she sat, this time with a smile that was more like a smirk, eyebrows raised with her head cocked sideways, as if to say: "Want to try again?" Smirking right back, I took off on one of two trails, this time of my own choosing. I didn't look back, and I didn't mind if she saw me with a moderate jog. I didn't break into a full run, partly because the trail had become much steeper, but also because I didn't want this funny little old lady with a great sense of humor to have a heart attack.

Well, you guessed it! Another clearing and there she sat, looking peaceful, breathing normally. As I approached, walking slowly and trying to breathe more slowly, she actually broke into a roar of laughter! Not knowing the Korean culture well enough, I was torn between a desire to laugh out loud and hug her, or to get down on my knees and bow repeatedly. I chose a most respectful half-bow and a gentle laugh of surrender. I also gestured with the palms of my hands together over my heart as if in prayer, followed by an extension of my hands and arms out and open toward her. No words were needed. She knew that I had been humbled, had a sense of humor, and that I was releasing a caring open heart to her.

There was one more path, thankfully the last, leading up to the top of the hill. We walked side by side with only an occasional glance and a giggle to the top. No words were spoken or needed.

Once there, we walked silently around the perimeter of a groomed space about fifty feet in diameter. My new friend stopped after a while, stood near the middle of what I assumed was a sacred site, closed her eyes, and spoke softly in Korean. She delivered a brief prayer. I felt that she might enjoy some time alone, and so I backed away slowly. As she glanced over at me, I used hand gestures and facial expression to show my admiration for her tender ways, her sense of humor, and with a laugh, her amazing physical strength. She returned a smile and a nod of agreement.

Two souls played, laughed, and shared heart-felt emotions that day, leaving me with what seemed another important clue that we really are all *one*.

13

Nuggets of Gold

The following three exchanges with our youngest son Andrew were nuggets of gold from the start. Their value increased beyond measure as the years flew by. I share them now for two reasons: They fit as pieces of the puzzle about which this book is written, and they reveal how profound insights about life, love, and courage may emerge when and where we least expect them.

Andrew and his older brother Matthew always enjoyed bubble stories, as we called them, at bedtime. We could climb into an imaginary bubble capable of travel underwater, to other countries, and to distant planets at nearly the speed of light. The bubble was impenetrable. We could miniaturize and travel within parts of the body and travel back in time or to the future. With eyes closed and mind and body in a meditative state, those stories put little kids in a sleepy mood, while allowing the older kid (me) to get creative and sneak in lessons about respect and good behavior. The bubble story, at times, would end with participants in transition toward complete peaceful sleep—sometimes including the storyteller!

You are now ready for the first nugget, an exchange one night at the end of a bubble trip when Andrew was slipping toward dreamland.

NUGGET 1

Sitting on the edge of his bed, nearly drifting off myself, I was brought fully awake when a deep masculine voice blurted out, "Dad, I am so glad I chose you and Mom." I turned and looked at my son, shocked by the tone and words leaving his lips. Even more amazing was the subtle facial change as he spoke, looking serious and beyond the features of a normal five-year-old child. It took all I could muster to simply respond by saying *"What?!"* He immediately replied with the same tone of an older, wiser person: "Dad, I am so glad I chose you and Mom." Now, having had a few seconds to gather my wits and search for a meaningful response, I managed a profound *"Why?!"*

And without hesitation, that seemingly aged and wise little guy said, "Because this time we have so much to learn."

I sat stunned and shaken for several minutes as I watched the face of our youngest little man return to a relaxed childlike expression. He and I had never discussed reincarnation or any other topics on the possible choice souls might have involving their parents. My father's encounter with his deceased brother and the "light" (chapter 10, "Love and Learn") played havoc with my mind as I tried to process the content and tone of Andrew's comments.

The information given my father while on the other side involving self-assessment and the reasons we return to earth filled my mind. I thought about the lessons my dad spoke of during our last night together, how important it is to learn and evolve as spirits, and how important it was to have closure in our relationship. These thoughts and my own close encounters with death raced through my mind. They all seemed divinely linked to this new disclosure that "this time we have so much to learn."

Later that evening I wrote down the exact words used by Andrew. I felt that there had been a rare and unexplainable connection of our souls. The very next day I asked Andrew if he had any memory of the words we shared that night. He did not and does not to this day. However, we have both come to appreciate the lessons about which he spoke on that memorable night. He, like his siblings, have brought so much love, fun, and excitement to our family. But there have also been a number of frightening, painful, expensive, and life-changing events, especially with Andrew! My wife and I continue to marvel over, and even enjoy, the fulfillment of Andrew's childhood warning.

NUGGET 2

One night just one year later when Andrew was six, the bedtime bubble story had been completed. Andrew was tucked in, wide awake, and looking like something was still on his mind. As I stood and prepared to launch the usual good-night routine, there was a last-minute request: "Dad, can you spend another minute or two?" Anxious to oblige, I returned to my usual position on the edge of his bed. Without a second of hesitation, he said, "What is infinity?" His pronunciation was off a bit, but I knew what he was trying to say. He said that his teacher had used the word but did not explain very well what it meant.

I sat quietly for a minute thinking about the best way to answer his question. My first attempt involved a discussion about earth, the sun, our galaxy, and eventually the existence of other galaxies that go on and on, never running out of room for more suns and planets. I hadn't even gotten to the infinite-space part when it was clear that my approach was a total bust. His half-closed eyes confirmed my failure.

The second try was better. He already knew how to count to 100, so I asked if he knew what comes after 100. He guessed that you just start over again. I explained that in a way you do but that you keep track of the numbers already counted. We counted together to 100 and then to the exciting discovery of 101, 102, etc. He stuck with me all the way to 200, 201, 202 . . . when he shouted, "Daddy, this is boring! When do you tell me about infinity?" I told him that we were getting to that and to try and be patient. To my surprise, he allowed me to count to 300, after which I explained how the process would continue through the hundreds all the way to a new level called one thousand.

He thought that was neat and asked if there were other levels after a thousand. The discussion went on for as long as I dared, with examples of hundreds of thousands and even thousands of thousands called millions. Fortunately, it was at this point that he asked if the levels ever ended. I said no and that if you wanted you could go on counting your entire life and never reach the last biggest number possible.

I could see the amazement in his eyes as he attempted to understand how something could continue to get bigger and bigger and never end. I jumped in for the opportunity of the moment and told him that there were other things that, like numbers, could go on without end. I said that there was a name for that unimaginable greatest condition, and that it is "infinity."

Andrew paused. He thought for a moment and then said the most joyful words any parent could ever hope to hear: "Daddy, that's how much I love you! I love you infinity!" The grammar wasn't perfect, but the message was. Those words were, and remain to this day, a priceless gift. They still bring about the happiest tears whenever he, his wife, and any of my kids say: "Dad, we love you infinity."

NUGGET 3

The sharing of this experience is important because it gave me the courage to write this book. It involves another bedtime exchange between Andrew and me when he was seven years of age. We had just finished a wonderful journey in our imaginary bubble, when out of the blue, Andrew asked if I knew what a soul is. I was pleased that he had come up with such a great question. But I struggled with an explanation that would best fit the mind of a second-grade student. The struggle, of course, was more accurately tied to the fact that I didn't know the answer.

I tried to explain that people are much more than their physical bodies and that a special non-physical gift from God, something we call our soul, lives within each of us. I fumbled with concepts of consciousness and the role our brains play in gathering information, making decisions, and remembering things we do. I suggested that all we do, say, and think about may be saved within our consciousness as part of our soul, even after we die.

I thought I was on a roll that would satisfy his curiosity when he interrupted with: "Dad, I've been thinking about this a lot today, and I think I figured it out." Surprised and also relieved, I asked if he would like to share his thoughts.

The answer was an eager "*Yes!*" as he sat up straight, repositioned his pillow, and suggested that a soul is like a bundle of energy. It is sort of round, like a ball with a bumpy surface. As he spoke, his hands created the size, shape, and surface of the bundle he was describing. He went on with excitement in his voice, face, and hand gestures telling me just how special that ball of energy is. He stopped for minute, looked off toward the ceiling, and then continued with why that bundle of energy was so special. He told me that the bundle, the soul, is special because of what it contains. I remember him asking with a mischievous smile, head straight ahead, a glance toward me from the corners of his eyes: "Do you know what a soul is made of?" I humbly responded with: "No, I guess I don't."

Now, at this point, he already had me at "a bundle of energy," and I could hardly wait for the next hunk of wisdom. He looked straight at me and with confidence said, "It is made of love and courage"—his exact words! He waited patiently as I tried to clear my throat, retain dry eyes, and come up with some meaningful response. I failed. Worse yet, I started to get up while thanking him for his fantastic description of a soul. My desire to say more was quickly interrupted by a sharp, almost father-like scolding asking, "Dad, don't you wonder *why* a soul is made of love and courage?"

Oh boy, I was probably thinking how in just ten years I'm going to tell this guy, "No, you can't have the car tonight!" I returned to my seat at the edge of his bed and told him that yes, I really do wonder why. Yielding no forgiveness for my attempted premature departure, he said, "Well, if you think about it, the answer is clear. The only thing that matters in this world is love, but it takes a lot of courage to show it."

Those words of Andrew's have helped me in countless ways since that night. I could write another book on just that piece of wisdom and the seemingly infinite ways it has helped me overcome fears, deal with difficult people, and face my own shortcomings with love of self.

If the answer "to love and learn" given to my father for why we come to earth is combined with the nugget of gold presented here, the result would be to *love and learn with courage*. To do so would more than light the way; it could actually be the way while discovering the "soul" purpose for one's life.

Final Thoughts

There are countless uncertainties about the interconnectedness of body, mind, and spirit. My life events selected for this book do not provide answers for those uncertainties. They do, however, provide situations, discoveries, and lessons that have caused me to pause and explore the most intriguing connections involving my body, my brain, and that which could survive the end of life—consciousness.

I often marveled over the continued protection and survival of my body throughout my life. I wondered why I had survived, why moments of clarity and calm had overtaken me at just the right moments, and how unexplainable interventions had kept me alive. I grew increasingly curious about a non-physical part of my being, or consciousness—something apart from my brain that seemed to be connected with intelligence and purpose beyond this world. A window of insight was opening about my life journey. I was recognizing clues about the path I was on and about the greatest puzzle of all—the purpose for my life and what could come next.

My close encounters with death or serious injury were near-drownings, impacts with vehicles, extreme freezing conditions, and even moose mercy. The full significance of each event was often missed or not yet understood in my early youth. It was only after repeated survivals that I began to ask, "Why me?" When I had already experienced the loss of good friends in their youth, it didn't seem right that I should be spared.

The concept that there might be something I am supposed to learn or do was confusing and hard to accept. I was well into my studies and profession involving scientific process, principles, and proof. There was little room in my world for the possible intent of mysterious, unexplainable events. Intent, I felt, included the monitoring and control of exposures I might need or deserve in order to progress toward some goal in my lifetime.

My attempts to understand so many close calls were further complicated by unimaginable experiences involving premonitions, a period of depression, and many perfectly timed connections with people and events. Whether a simple sharing of appreciation and respect, a challenge of the existence of God, or a sharing of my father's life-after-death experience, each event opened my heart and my mind to the possibility that we are all connected.

My interest in religion—any belief rigidly founded upon a single church, faith, or way to worship—was losing ground to a growing need to feel connected spiritually with all living things: people, plants, and animals. I was gradually accepting the fact that I would never find scientific proof that an all-knowing source of love and creative power was behind all this, but the clues for such continued to impact my life.

It was clear to me that even the strongest of clues for enlightenment were not evidence or *proof* that God exists, that there is a spiritually guided path for my life, or that I will even exist after I die. However, the events did provide incentive and guidance for me to remain steadfast and confident that I had come into this life with a purpose.

Most of my life I thought that my primary goal was to work as a specialist for the prevention and control of oil spills. As exciting as that career was, and as helpful I believe it was for the environment, I now see that there was an even greater purpose for my involvement. Along with the mission to prevent spillage and protect the environment was the unique opportunity to learn how to love and respect all creatures that use and depend upon that environment. The path for that learning seemed long and difficult at times, but the pieces for the puzzle of my own life purpose began to fit together.

I finally realized that it is not the amount or duration of purpose I fulfill in this life, but the realization that there *is* a purpose for each of us. That purpose, I believe, is to discover and use the capacity we each have to love and learn in our own unique way with courage to stay the course.

The events presented in this book, their lessons, and the encounters I've had with family, friends, and others around the world lead me to believe that a most important part of my mission was and still is to spread joyful hope for the purpose of life and what could follow. This book, I believe, is part of that mission.

About the Author

A lan A. Allen, born in New Jersey in 1938, always loved science. He graduated from Washington & Jefferson College in Pennsylvania as a physics major, spent five years in the U.S. Navy, and continued studies at several universities in physics, petroleum engineering, and oceanography. In 2020 he retired from a career as a world-renowned oil spill specialist that took him to dozens of countries and involved working closely with governments, academic institutions, private industry, and most major oil companies.

He developed new technology and equipment for the prevention and control of spills and conducted studies of pollution impacts on marine and inland environments. His accomplishments include an industry/agency Legacy Award, a Meritorious Public Service Award, three patents for spill control systems, and recognition as an aquanaut during the early stages of the Hydro-Lab program.

Mr. Allen says that while his work as a scientist was rewarding, his most fascinating experiences were those that challenged science, often involved unexplainable events, and provided clues for life's purpose. His greatest satisfaction is living long enough to write this book and share his findings for why we are here and what could be next.

Printed in the United States
By Bookmasters